QUESTIONS & ANSWERS:
Torts

Multiple Choice and Short Answer
Questions and Answers

By

Anita Bernstein
Sam Nunn Professor of Law
Emory University

and

David P. Leonard
Professor of Law and William M. Rains Fellow
Loyola Law School

LexisNexis

ISBN#: 08205-5667-X

Editorial Offices
744 Broad Street, Newark, NJ 07102 (973) 820-2000
201 Mission St., San Francisco, CA 94105-1831 (415) 908-3200
701 East Water Street, Charlottesville, VA 22902-7587 (434) 972-7600
www.lexis.com

(Pub.3181)

Anita Bernstein, Sam Nunn Professor of Law at Emory University, has also taught at Chicago-Kent, Cornell, Fordham, Iowa, Michigan, and Seton Hall law schools. She has taught Torts for fifteen years and recently served as chair of the Torts & Compensation Systems section of the Association of American Law Schools. She has published extensively on the relation between torts and other subjects, including feminist theory, comparative law, and the sociology of products liability.

David P. Leonard is Professor of Law and William M. Rains Fellow at Loyola Law School, Los Angeles. Prior to joining the Loyola faculty in 1991, he was Professor of Law at Indiana University School of Law - Indianapolis. He has taught Torts for more than twenty years and is the author of numerous law review articles and several books, including another book in this series, *Questions & Answers: Evidence*.

The law of torts is designed to deal with an extremely broad range of human conduct, from punches in the nose to automobile accidents; from affronts to dignity to environmental pollution; from defective products to fraud. Not only must rules of tort law regulate vastly different types of potentially harmful behavior, but they must also be flexible enough to account for the almost limitless variety of fact patterns within each type. To put it simply, no two punches in the nose are exactly alike. And yet, the rules must be fashioned in such a way as to make the law at least reasonably predictable, and the results of the cases both fair to individuals and conducive to social prosperity.

For these reasons, modern rules of tort law are written in broad strokes. They do not seek to prescribe specific behavior in specific circumstances (always stop, look, and listen before crossing a railroad track). Rather, they set forth general principles to guide behavior in a variety of circumstances (always exercise reasonable care). Thus, instead of purporting to tell us exactly what to do, they provide us with standards against which our conduct may be measured.

The very generality of tort rules is what makes the study of tort law difficult. But it is not unstructured. Every claim for relief, and every affirmative defense, has a set of required *elements*. These elements tell lawyers what they must allege and prove in order to demonstrate their clients' entitlement to relief or, respectively, why their clients should not be held responsible. It is the student's task to learn what these elements are and to develop an understanding about how to apply them to real and hypothetical fact patterns.

How can *Questions and Answers: Torts* help you in this task? Recognizing that torts coverage varies somewhat from school to school and even from day to day in the same course, this book follows a comparably varied path to give you what you need. You will find a range of difficulty here. Some questions are tough, while others are pretty easy. The multiple choice questions might ask you to pick the best of a list, the worst of a list, or the story that illustrates a point of doctrine most effectively, as well as other routes to mastery of the material. The short answers ask you to analyze scenarios and communicate discrete points. A little (simple) arithmetic comes up now and then— just as it does for practicing lawyers. The Practice Final Exam simulates the reality of a final exam by not announcing up-front, as the topic headings do, which tort is being tested. Whether you're in your beginning or ending stage of pulling torts material together, then, you'll find coverage at the appropriate level.

Like most torts classes, the book goes beyond "blackletter" material. While most of its questions use the familiar "issue-spotter" approach to doctrine—an approach you can probably expect to see on your final—a number of questions will help you review social policy, economic theory, fairness, and the insights of famed common law judges. Most torts teachers expect you to think about torts at this more conceptual level, while also mastering its rules and elements.

Despite its wide swath, this book is neither a casebook nor a treatise. Its purpose is to help you test your comprehension of the elements of the most important tort claims and defenses. We do not purport to teach you the law in the first instance; that is the purpose of your torts class. Therefore, you should not attempt to answer the questions in any particular part of this book until you have studied the applicable law in your torts class.

Once you have completed an area of study, you should work your way through the problems in that part of the book to test the depth of your understanding of the subject matter. Take your time. Try to answer each question before reviewing our answers and the explanations they provide. If the question calls for a written response, write something before reviewing the answer. Don't just think about what you might say.

When you reach the end of your torts class, you should take the Practice Final Exam. Give yourself 90 minutes to answer the 44 questions on that exam, and do so under simulated exam conditions. When you are finished, review the answers. This exercise should give you a better idea of how to allocate your study time before your actual final.

We have many people to thank for helping us to reach the point where we could put these questions before you with confidence that you will benefit from them. Above all, we thank our students who, over many years, have challenged us to dig deeper into the "whys" and "wherefores" of this fascinating subject. We also appreciate the assistance of Jack Glezen and Rhonda Heermans and wish to thank Professor Keith Rowley of the William S. Boyd School of Law, University of Nevada, Las Vegas, and Heather Dean and Mike Scalise, our editors at LexisNexis, for their help in finalizing the manuscript.

ANITA BERNSTEIN
Atlanta, Georgia

DAVID P. LEONARD
Los Angeles, California

December, 2003

TABLE OF CONTENTS

QUESTIONS

Starling arranged to undergo surgery. Lecter, her surgeon, did not inform Starling that he was HIV-positive because he genuinely believed it to be a private matter that posed no risk to Starling. Lecter carefully avoided cutting himself during surgery, and the surgery was successful. Six months after the surgery, however, Starling learned of Lecter's HIV status. She became extremely apprehensive, and took an HIV test, which, fortunately, proved to be negative. Nevertheless, the anxiety she suffered was extremely severe, and led to significant weight loss and other physical illness. Starling has contacted an attorney to determine whether she has a legal basis on which to pursue Lecter. The attorney is considering filing a battery claim on Starling's behalf against Lecter.

1.   Which of the following statements is most likely correct?

(A)   Because Starling was in need of, and consented to, the surgery, a battery claim will fail.

(B)   Because Lecter did not expose Starling to the HIV virus, a battery claim will fail.

(C)   Because Lecter has rights to privacy and self-determination, and because he still possesses a license to practice medicine, his decision not to inform Starling of his status would not be deemed unlawful. Thus, a battery claim will fail.

(D)   Because Starling's consent was not fully informed, the surgery constituted an offensive touching for which Lecter might be held liable in battery.

Herrle was a nurse's aide at a hospital that treated many Alzheimer's patients. Alzheimer's sufferers are often violent, and Herrle knew that her job involved working with violent, combative patients. Herrle also knew about past incidents in which patients attacked aides, but she and other aides received training in handling violent patients. Marshall was such a patient. On previous occasions, she had hit hospital employees, and her admitting diagnosis noted her aggressiveness and the high risk that she would cause injury. One day, Herrle saw that Marshall was being aggressive with another aide who was trying to move her from a chair into bed. Herrle entered the room to help because she was afraid Marshall would fall. While she was helping, Marshall hit Herrle several times on the head, causing serious injuries.

2.   Herrle wishes to sue Marshall for battery. Which of the following statements is most accurate?

(A)   Regardless of Marshall's actual intent, she will be held liable both to encourage her family to take better care of Marshall and to compensate an innocent plaintiff.

(B)   Even if Marshall's mental illness deprived her of control over her arm and hand when she struck Herrle, she will be liable.

(C) Even if Marshall's mental illness caused her to suffer the delusion that Herrle was attacking her, she will be liable.

(D) Because Marshall's mental illness removed any moral fault from her actions, she cannot be held liable for an intentional tort such as battery.

3. Can a defendant be liable for assault if in fact she is not capable of inflicting harmful contact on the plaintiff? Explain.

ANSWER:

Sam and Rebecca, teenagers in love, were playing tag in the park. Rebecca was "it," and within a few minutes caught Sam. Rather than lightly tapping him, however, she hit him in the jaw with her fist, breaking one of his teeth. She had not intended to break a tooth, only to smack him in fun. Sam sues Rebecca for battery to recover for his broken tooth.

4. Which of the following statements is most accurate?

(A) Sam will prevail because Rebecca, in exercising her right of self-defense, exceeded the force reasonably necessary to repel Sam's attack.

(B) Sam will prevail because Rebecca, by striking him so hard, exceeded the scope of his consent to a touching.

(C) Rebecca will prevail because, by agreeing to play the game, Sam consented to touches that would otherwise constitute batteries.

(D) Rebecca will prevail because she did not intend to break Sam's tooth.

Chloe and Pete, age 10, were playing tag in the park. Pete was "it," and was advancing on Chloe. In order to avoid being tagged by Pete, Chloe stood behind Karl, a bystander, and used him as a shield by keeping Karl between herself and Pete. As Pete closed in, Chloe gently pushed Karl toward Pete, hoping Pete would jump back and give Chloe a chance to escape. Karl stumbled and fell, suffering an injury. Karl sues Chloe for battery.

5. Which of the following arguments on Chloe's behalf has the greatest chance of success?

(A) Chloe should only be liable for nominal damages for the gentle push but not for damages for Karl's injury because she did not intend nor could she foresee such a result.

(B) Chloe should not be liable because a child of age 10 cannot form the requisite intent for battery.

(C) Chloe should not be liable because a gentle push cannot constitute a battery.

(D) Chloe should not be liable because a child on a playground has a privilege to touch a bystander, and even to give the person a gentle push.

6. Which of the following scenarios illustrates a claim for battery <u>without</u> an accompanying claim for assault?

    (A) Plaintiff Letitia, riding her motorcycle, was hit by motorist Mart and knocked unconscious. Dr. Doolittle, a physician who was walking near the scene of the accident, rendered emergency care to Letitia without her consent.

    (B) Before undergoing general anesthesia, plaintiff Sharon reached an agreement with her surgeon, Dr. Spurgeon, saying that she consented to having her appendix removed. Sharon consented to the removal of no other organs. While she was unconscious, Dr. Spurgeon removed her gallbladder as well.

    (C) Despite being a rich man, plaintiff Patrick habitually refused to pay his medical bills. His physician, Dr. Proctor, became infuriated by this practice. When Patrick lay on Dr. Proctor's examining table, Dr. Proctor brandished a scalpel and shouted, "I'm going to amputate your left eye!" Patrick was able to deflect Dr. Proctor with the help of a well-aimed judo chop.

    (D) Plaintiff Cankersore recovered slowly from a back injury with the help of painkillers, to which he became addicted. His treating physician, Dr. Horsefeathers, obtained sexual gratification from Cankersore by threatening to withhold prescriptions for the painkillers. Cankersore agreed to Dr. Horsefeathers's touchings, believing he would be in grave pain if he did not consent.

7. For purposes of intentional tort liability, what is the difference between intent and motive? Give an illustration, with reference to battery, where an actor could be found to have committed an intentional tort despite his or her praiseworthy motive.

ANSWER:

8. Is it possible for a three-year-old child to be liable for an intentional tort?

    (A) Yes, if her behavior manifests her intent.

    (B) Yes, if she is capable of verbal testimony.

    (C) No, because she is incapable of negligence.

    (D) No, because she is incompetent as a matter of law.

Siobhan, hating Puckaluck and wishing him dead, had no reason to have confidence in her bomb-building skills. She had flunked high school chemistry. Nevertheless, she found on the Internet a set of directions for making a crude explosive device, and followed them as best as she could to create a letter bomb. She mailed Puckaluck this letter bomb, laughing at herself for attempting such a futile experiment. Against all odds, the letter bomb exploded in Puckaluck's hands, killing him.

9. Can Siobhan be liable to Puckaluck's estate for battery?

   (A) Yes, because Siobhan's purpose is sufficient to establish intent, and she fulfilled the other requirements of battery as well.

   (B) Yes, because Siobhan acted with substantial certainty, and she fulfilled the other requirements of battery as well.

   (C) No, because, although Siobhan's actions fulfilled elements of a battery claim, Siobhan lacked substantial certainty that harmful contact would result.

   (D) No, because, although Siobhan's actions fulfilled the elements of a battery claim, causation in fact is absent.

10. For purposes of liability for assault, what is the difference between fear and apprehension?
ANSWER:

After Robert began to act strangely, his parents took him to Southwood Psychiatric Center (Southwood), where they met with Sara, a psychiatrist. During the interview, Robert expressed suicidal thoughts and also threatened to kill both his parents and his brother's murderers. Sara concluded that Robert was intoxicated, out of control, very depressed, suicidal, angry, hostile, and agitated. She also concluded that Robert posed a danger to himself and others, and that he should be detained for 72 hours pursuant to a state statute. When she informed Robert of this, Robert said these conclusions were not accurate, and he tried to leave. His parents pulled him away from the door to stop him and yelled, "close the door." Reuben, a nurse who did not yet know about Robert, closed the door, leaving Robert inside. Robert then walked to the lobby elevator. An alert was called, and several employees, including Reuben, responded. Sara notified the employees that Robert was dangerous and that they should escort him upstairs. When the employees saw Robert, Robert moved toward them, stating, "Come on, I'll take you all on," and began to remove his jacket. He swore at his parents, yelled, "I'm going to kill them," and said he wanted to die. The employees believed Robert was dangerous and physically restrained him. The staff then completed the necessary forms, and Robert was admitted. At this point, the formal 72-hour hold began.

11. Robert claims that, although the 72-hour hold might have been legal, he was falsely imprisoned prior to the time the statutory hold officially began. Of the following, which argument provides the strongest defense to Robert's false imprisonment claim?

    (A) Assuming Southwood personnel were following statutory procedures in assessing Robert's condition, his detention prior to the initiation of the 72-hour hold was not unlawful.

    (B) Because Southwood personnel did not intend to detain Robert until the initiation of the 72-hour hold, they did not possess the necessary intent for false imprisonment.

    C) Because Robert was not physically restrained prior to the initiation of the 72-hour hold, he was not falsely imprisoned.

    (D) Because Robert was allowed to move freely within the building prior to the initiation of the 72-hour hold, he was not falsely imprisoned.

During a commercial flight, one of the plane's three engines stopped working. The captain truthfully assured the passengers that the plane could fly safely on its remaining engines and announced that the plane would continue to its scheduled destination. One of the passengers, Frank, was not reassured, and demanded that the plane land at the first available airport. The captain refused, even though the plane's flight path would take it close to another airport. The plane continued on course and landed on time an hour later at its scheduled destination. Frank sues the airline for false imprisonment.

12.   Of the following, which constitutes the airline's strongest defense?

(A) Because the plane landed on time at its original destination, there was no confinement.

(B) Because Frank was the only passenger who wanted to land earlier, to have done so would have falsely imprisoned all the other passengers by taking them where they did not want to go.

(C) Frank's confinement was not unlawful.

(D) Frank was not physically harmed by the confinement.

Grudgepudge, a Web designer, accepted an offer from Sam to visit Sam's home office. The purpose of this meeting was for Sam to consider hiring Grudgepudge to design a new website for Sam's business. Grudgepudge brought his laptop computer to the meeting and demonstrated some interactive features of websites that Grudgepudge had designed. About an hour into the meeting, Grudgepudge excused himself to make several business calls to other clients of his, using his cell phone. When he returned to Sam's office, Sam smirked, "Soooo — where's your laptop, buddy?" Grudgepudge looked around; it was not in sight. Sam had hidden the laptop somewhere in his office while Grudgepudge was away. Grudgepudge demanded to know why Sam had hidden the laptop, but Sam refused to answer. Grudgepudge remained at Sam's office for another two hours, attempting to regain his laptop.

13.   An action by Grudgepudge against Sam for false imprisonment should

(A) fail, because Sam had a privilege to claim temporary possession of Grudgepudge's laptop.

(B) fail, because Sam did not confine Grudgepudge.

(C) succeed, because Sam wrongfully withheld Grudgepudge's property and departing from Sam's office would have meant leaving the laptop behind.

(D) succeed, because Sam had no privilege to claim temporary possession of Grudgepudge's property and Grudgepudge felt reasonable compulsion to remain.

Rhonda and Remus, teenage hikers, came upon a small abandoned barn. While Rhonda explored the interior of the barn, climbing into a hayloft, Remus explored the exterior. He noticed that a horizontal two-by-four slab of wood could seal the only door to the barn from the outside, preventing anyone inside the barn from exiting. Moving this slab into place, Remus locked Rhonda into the barn and called good-bye to her, ignoring her cries for help and pleas for release. Hoping to gain the attention of a potential rescuer, Rhonda leaned into a crack in the barn wall, calling out for help. About a half-hour after Remus walked away, passerby Pia heard Rhonda's cries, but decided to ignore them.

14. An action by Rhonda against Pia for false imprisonment should fail because

(A) Pia did not imprison Rhonda.

(B) Remus is the proper defendant for a claim of false imprisonment.

(C) Rhonda entered the barn voluntarily.

(D) Rhonda was a trespasser.

Store detective Escamillo observes Gretchen slip five compact discs from a display shelf into her large leather purse. The discs contain recorded music and are priced at $14.99 each. Gretchen is about to walk out the store door into a crowded parking lot. Escamillo wishes to protect the store's property but does not want to be liable, or make his employer liable, for the tort of false imprisonment.

15. How should he proceed?
ANSWER:

Marylebone Island, a small, rustic bit of land connected to a mainland town only by a rickety bridge, attracts occasional explorers. Hurley was fond of driving her fifteen-year-old automobile over the bridge and strolling around the island. Her enemy, Hommyside, decided to kill her by connecting a bomb to her automobile ignition while Hurley was away exploring the island. Hommyside's plan was that, on her return, Hurley would turn the ignition key and the bomb would go off, killing her. The plan didn't work. Between the time that Hommyside wired the explosive and Hurley's return to her car, a severe storm pounded Marylebone Island. Because of the age of the car, the hood was not watertight. Rainwater got under the hood, ruining Hommyside's rewiring. When Hurley attempted to start her car, the wet, exposed ignition wires would not send current to the engine and the car simply failed to start, trapping Hurley on Marylebone Island for several hours.

16. Has Hommyside's conduct fulfilled a prima facie case for false imprisonment?

(A) Yes, because Hommyside's rewiring created a physical barrier that confined Hurley to Marylebone Island.

(B) Yes, under transferred intent: Homyside intended to commit a battery and the consequences of false imprisonment resulted.

(C) No, because Hommyside intended harmful bodily contact, not unlawful confinement.

(D) No, because Hurley voluntarily entered the island and assumed the risk of automobile failure.

17. Which of the following invasions would NOT be actionable under the tort of trespass to land?

(A) Sound engineer/computer programmer Klutzmonkey experiments with digital recordings of harsh-sounding musical instruments, trying to write programming code that captures the range of what these bizarre instruments produce. In these experiments, Klutzmonkey makes unpleasant sounds that disturb his neighbors.

(B) Motivated by malice, Yodel removes the lids of his filled trash cans and lays the cans on their sides, hoping that the wind will blow his trash onto the lawn of his neighbor. It does.

(C) In a chic urban brownstone district, Adele, Bittybop, and Chichi own adjacent houses. Each lot is only 20 feet wide. Adele and Chichi have been living there for years; Bittybop recently moved into the middle house. In the back of their houses, Adele and Chichi like to toss a football from Adele's lot to Chichi's lot and back. Their ability to throw a football has improved, and ever since Bittybop moved in, the ball has never landed in Bittybop's yard.

(D) The Historic Pumpkinsburg Association, Inc. (HPA), an incorporated neighborhood association in the town of Pumpkinsburg, asked homeowner Derrick Dingaling if he would be willing to hang the HPA flag from his flagpole during Civic Pride Week, running from October 17-24. Dingaling told the HPA staff that he would be willing to fly this flag during this week provided that HPA would assume responsibility for removing the flag on October 25. It is now October 28 and HPA still has done nothing to remove the flag.

One bright Sunday afternoon, automobile drivers Gallant and Mordred both found themselves on the property of Landholder in their separate cars. Gallant had entered Landholder's land on purpose, knowing that it belonged to Landholder and not to Gallant. His motive for entering was to explore the property and see if he wanted to make an offer to buy it. Mordred, by contrast, had entered Landholder's land by accident. Mordred had become distracted while quarreling over the telephone with his wife, and steered to the left instead of to the right. Steering to the right would have brought him onto his own adjacent property had he been paying attention to his driving. Assume that both automobiles caused some grass to be pressed down but otherwise caused no damages to Landholder.

18. Discuss Landholder's potential claims against Gallant and Mordred.
ANSWER:

College student Cindy uses an old laptop computer with an archaic operating system. Despite some teasing from her social circle, she is content with this laptop. One of her friends, Francine, could not imagine how any laptop user could tolerate such low speed, poor screen resolution, and frequent system failures. One day when she knew Cindy was in class and not using the laptop, Francine went to Cindy's dormitory room. Francine told Cindy's roommate that she had come to upgrade Cindy's laptop. "About time," said the roommate, admitting Francine to the room. Francine remained there, installing the new system. She had it ready to go by the time Cindy returned from class. Much to Francine's disappointment, Cindy expressed displeasure about Francine's behavior. It turned out that Cindy had planned to enter her laptop in a competition called "The World's Greatest Clunker," which featured prizes in various categories for archaic computers. Cindy can prove that she probably would have won.

19. Does Cindy have a tort claim against Francine?

(A) No, because any potential claim is eliminated by the roommate's consent.

(B) No, because Cindy experienced only benefit, and no detriment, from Francine's behavior.

(C) Yes, for trespass to chattels, if Francine's upgrade lowered the value of the laptop in the "World's Greatest Clunker" competition.

(D) Yes, for trespass to land, if Cindy can establish that the roommate did not have authority to approve entry to the dormitory room for this purpose.

20. Which of the following is NOT an example of a behavior that can constitute conversion?

(A) Wrongful transfer

(B) Negligent alteration

(C) Theft

(D) Bona fide purchase of stolen goods

21. Describe the types of property that are covered under the tort of conversion and the types of property that are not.

ANSWER:

Well after midnight, the night manager of the Empire Hotel got a call from the River City Police Department (RCPD) informing her that Pushkin, a hotel guest, was a terrorist. The caller asked the manager to detain Pushkin for a few hours until the police could arrange a reliable and safe way to arrest him. The manager agreed. From the late hour, the manager assumed that Pushkin was in the room. She then locked what she believed to be Pushkin's door from the outside. Two hours later, she discovered that she had locked the door to Peter's room instead of Pushkin's. Peter slept through the whole thing, but when he found out that he'd been locked in his room, he sued the Empire Hotel for false imprisonment.

22. Which of the following statements is correct?

(A) Peter will prevail because he was actually confined.

(B) Peter will prevail if his distress on learning of his prior confinement was severe.

(C) Peter will lose because he was unaware of the confinement until later, and he suffered no physical harm as a result of his confinement.

(D) Peter will lose because the manager did not intend to confine him.

Penny operated a small custom jewelry store on the 10th floor of an older building. One evening after closing time, Dougray broke into the store to steal jewelry. When he unexpectedly discovered that Penny was still there, Dougray cut the phone lines, took the jewelry, and left. He then barricaded the door from the outside so that Penny would be unable to leave the store. When Penny found she couldn't open the door, she sat down and prepared for a long night. There was a fire escape just outside the window in Penny's store, but Penny did not use it because she was afraid of heights. By sheer coincidence, an employee came by about an hour later to retrieve something he'd forgotten. He cleared the barricades and freed Penny. Penny sues Dougray for false imprisonment.

23. Which of the following statements is correct?

(A) Penny's action will fail because her confinement was too short to constitute false imprisonment.

(B) Penny's action will fail because she failed to use a reasonable means of escape.

(C) Penny's action will fail because she suffered no harm.

(D) Penny has a strong false imprisonment case.

When Potter stopped his car at a red light, Denny ran up to the car, forced open the driver's door, ordered Potter to move over, and got in. He then brandished a knife and ordered Potter to turn over his wallet and get out. Potter refused, and started screaming for help. Denny then, with Potter in the passenger seat, took off. Potter remained in the car even when Denny had to stop several times for traffic lights. Finally, Denny abandoned the car in a remote location with Potter still inside.

24. If Potter sues Denny for false imprisonment, which of the following statements is correct?

(A) Potter has a strong false imprisonment case.

(B) Potter's case is weak because he chose to remain in the car rather than follow Denny's order to turn over the wallet.

(C) Potter's case is weak because the more appropriate action is for assault.

(D) Potter's case will fail because the more appropriate action is for conversion.

Driving home from work one day through a rural area, Pasha found the road blocked by Davidson Construction Co., which was renovating a house and had placed equipment and supplies on the road. Davidson did not have a permit to block the road. When Pasha asked Davidson personnel to move the equipment, the construction foreperson refused, telling Pasha that she could take another route. The only other route required a five-mile detour. Pasha reluctantly took that alternate route, but has now consulted you about suing Davidson for false imprisonment.

25. Evaluate the possible claim.

ANSWER:

After Emily nearly ran June down with her car, Emily pulled the car to the curb and got out. As she approached June, June moved toward her with her fists in the air, and yelled, "If you weren't bigger than me, I'd punch your lights out right now!" Emily believed June was going to hit her, and struck first, breaking June's nose. In fact, June only intended to argue with Emily, not to punch her.

26. If June sues Emily for battery to recover for the broken nose, which of the following is most likely correct?

(A) Because June's words conveyed her intention not to punch Emily, the court should rule as a matter of law that Emily did not have a privilege to punch June first.

(B) Even though June's words conveyed her intention not to punch Emily, the court should permit the jury to decide whether Emily was privileged to punch June first.

(C) If, due to their difference in size, June did not have the apparent means to hurt Emily, Emily had no privilege to punch June first.

(D) If Emily intended to harm June, Emily will be liable as a matter of law.

27. If consent to what would otherwise be an intentional tort is obtained by the defendant's fraud, is the consent invalid, so that the prima facie case for an intentional tort remains and the defendant is liable?

ANSWER:

One rainy evening, George, who was recovering from a severe heart attack, went to the local multiplex to see "Screech 2," a scary movie. During a particularly tense moment, when the slasher was stalking one of his young victims in a dark house, Elaine, who was sitting behind George, tapped George's shoulder to ask the time. Believing he was being attacked, George reached into his pocket, withdrew a switchblade, and swung it behind him, slashing Elaine's arm.

28. If Elaine sues George for battery, which of the following arguments offers George a reasonable chance of avoiding liability?

(A) If George reasonably believed Elaine was attacking him, he acted in justifiable self-defense.

(B) Because of his state of mind, George was afflicted by temporary insanity, and cannot be held liable.

(C) Because George's reaction to Elaine's touch was not volitional, there was no "act," and George cannot be held liable.

(D) Because George's heart attack deprived him of the ability to control his movements, he cannot be held liable.

29.   Give an example of the privilege of public necessity and describe the legal consequences of this privilege.

ANSWER:

30.   Which of the following scenarios illustrates express consent to an act that would otherwise be actionable as an intentional tort?

(A) Stage magician Gethsemane asks the audience for a volunteer to lie down inside a wooden coffin and have the lid lowered. Volunteer Victor gets into the coffin and leaps out instantly, having discovered that the bottom of the coffin is lined with spikes. Victor brings an action against Gethsemane for battery.

(B) Bodybuilder Jane, proud of her abdominal muscles, invites Ralph to swing back and punch her with all his might. Ralph does so. Jane is for the most part unharmed, although the punch leaves her out of breath and a little sore for a few minutes. Jane brings an action against Ralph for battery.

(C) Nurse Nottingham comes to office worker Dilbert's cubicle and asks Dilbert if he wants to be vaccinated against influenza. Dilbert, wearing a T-shirt and talking on the phone, raises his left arm. Nottingham infers that Dilbert has consented, and injects him. It turns out that Dilbert did not want to be vaccinated. Dilbert brings an action against Nottingham for battery.

(D) Easley is a commercial cultivator of roses. A path through some of his plants, on his property, has become a kind of informal shortcut for children headed from middle school to a soccer field. Easley has long been aware of this entry into his land, and never stopped the children from taking this shortcut. Easley now brings an action against the children for trespass to land.

Following a verbal dispute about the relative merits of two professional football teams, Rupert and Hannah engaged in a fistfight in an alleyway behind a bar. They pounded at each other until the police arrived. The police arrested them both for assault and disturbance of the peace. Both were injured by the other's blows.

31. Discuss their tort claims with reference to battery and consent.

ANSWER:

32. In each of the following scenarios, suppose that the individual whose name begins the scenario is the plaintiff in a battery action. In which of them would the principle of consent implied by law suggest that the defendant ought to prevail?

    (A) Adam, playing football for his high school team, was tackled by opposing lineman Tacky and suffered injury.

    (B) Belinda's ophthalmologist asked her, during a routine eye examination, whether she would be willing to have the thickness of her cornea measured. This measure had no therapeutic benefit to Belinda; the ophthalmologist was measuring all the corneas that came into the office in the hopes of correlating corneal thickness with other variables for a research study. Belinda agreed to the measuring. Belinda now believes that the measuring injured her eye.

    (C) Currey gave consent for a hernia operation to Dr. Spongebath, a surgeon. Currey gave no other express consent. Dr. Spongebath not only operated on Currey's hernia but also removed Currey's gallbladder.

    (D) Dauphine became unconscious while riding an escalator and collapsed into the steps. She appeared not to be breathing and had only a faint pulse when a physician's assistant, Pallowag, standing on the escalator nearby, saw her collapse. Pallowag carried Dauphine off the escalator and applied mouth-to-mouth resuscitation.

    Late one night, a sneak thief named Rugrat broke a window to enter the home of Joplin, a bachelor who lived alone. Rugrat used a chisel to gain entry. Holding the chisel, Rugrat began roaming through Joplin's dark house, hoping to spot a wallet or a purse in easy view. Joplin was awakened by the noise and, reaching for a pistol he kept under his bed, walked to the door of his bedroom. Joplin saw Rugrat just as a beam of light from the street illuminated the chisel. Joplin thought the chisel was a handgun and promptly shot Rugrat in the chest, injuring Rugrat severely.

33. In a battery action by Rugrat against Joplin, Joplin ought to prevail because

    (A) although Joplin had a duty to retreat before injuring Rugrat preemptively, Joplin fulfilled this duty by remaining inside his bedroom.

    (B) Joplin had no duty to retreat and reasonably believed that Rugrat threatened his life.

    (C) Joplin did not have the mental state to sustain a prima facie claim of battery by Rugrat.

    (D) Rugrat's status on the land was that of a criminal trespasser.

Tort law has long taken an interest in "spring guns" and similar devices that protect unoccupied property by setting up a tripwire that an intruder sets off when he or she crosses some threshold. By rigging the wire to some firearm, the property owner can arrange for the intruder to be shot before he or she can enter. Tort law generally frowns on this self-help measure. Suppose no liability rules exist on the subject. For this question you are free to write your own doctrine.

34.   In which of the following settings would a spring-gun trap for intruders make the most sense, suggesting a relatively good case for no liability to intruders who get injured while invading?

(A)   A remote, unoccupied building containing valuable physical items.

(B)   A home with vulnerable family members living inside.

(C)   A commercial warehouse amenable to private patrols by security personnel.

(D)   An abandoned house that drug users have taken over for sales and shelter.

Imagine the following split-second scenario as if you had time to weigh all your options: You are in a cocktail lounge and you see a person at the crowded bar slipping a vial of some liquid into another person's drink, while the person about to drink is not looking. The person about to drink lifts her cocktail glass by the stem and opens her mouth, preparing to drink.

35.   Does tort doctrine permit you to use force, or any kind of physical contact, to defend the drinker before she drinks the adulterated cocktail? If so, consider what you could do that would be both privileged and effective, and also state which tort(s) you could be accused of committing.

ANSWER:

Law school buddies Adam and Eve scaled a construction fence intending to play a prank by spray-painting one of the construction vehicles. While on the construction site, Adam fell and hit the ground hard, knocking himself out. Seeing this, Eve ran away because she didn't want to be caught. She did not report the accident, and Adam was not discovered until the next morning, when a construction worker found him on the ground. By that time, Adam had suffered additional injury from exposure. Adam has sued Eve for negligence, claiming that she should have assisted him.

36. Which of the following constitutes Adam's strongest argument for liability?

(A) Eve's going to the scene with Adam was an act of misfeasance for which she should be held liable.

(B) As a joint venturer, Eve is vicariously liable for the harm Adam suffered.

(C) Eve is in a special relationship with Adam as a result of their joint venture, imposing on her an obligation to take affirmative steps to assist Adam.

(D) Because the harm to Adam was the direct and proximate result of Eve's failure to assist him, Eve is liable.

Same facts as in Question 36. Sara, the construction worker who found Adam early in the morning, knew Adam was in need of medical care. Sara had arrived at the site before anybody else. She carefully placed Adam in the passenger seat of her pickup truck and headed for the nearest hospital. On the way, the pickup ran out of gas. Sara grabbed an empty gas can from the vehicle's bed, ran to a gas station, filled the can, and returned as quickly as she could, but the delay cost Adam more blood and led to further physical injury.

37. If Adam sues Sara, which of the following statements is most likely correct?

(A) Because Sara undertook to assist Adam, she was obligated to complete her rescue effort successfully. Her failure to do so will make her liable.

(B) Because Sara undertook to assist Adam, she was obligated to exercise reasonable care in the effort. If it was unreasonable to attempt to take Adam to the hospital in the pickup, Sara will be held liable for negligence.

(C) Because Sara undertook to assist Adam, she was obligated to exercise reasonable care in the effort. Sara was acting in an emergency situation, however, and cannot be held liable even though her pickup ran out of gas on the way to the hospital.

(D) Because Sara did not place Adam in his perilous position and had no special relationship with Adam, statutes in most jurisdictions provide that she will not be liable unless she intentionally harmed Adam during her rescue effort.

38. Courts sometimes hold that a defendant owes no duty to an "unforeseeable plaintiff." What is an unforeseeable plaintiff?

ANSWER:

Peter built a small pond in front of his house for his prize koi fish. The pond was visible from the sidewalk. To keep people and animals away, Peter constructed an eight-foot high chain link fence between the sidewalk and the pond. One day, Stewie, a particularly agile six-year-old who lived next door, struggled over the fence to get a closer look at the koi. When Stewie bent down to "pet" a fish, he fell into the water, hit his head on the bottom of the pond, and was rendered unconscious. Three minutes later, Lois, a passerby, saw Stewie floating in the pond, and climbed over the fence to rescue him. Stewie suffered permanent brain damage in the accident, and sues Peter for negligence. Assume these events took place in a state that has not abolished the common-law status categories for land entrants.

39. Which of the following statements is most likely correct?

(A) Because Stewie was a trespasser to whom Peter did not owe a duty of reasonable care with respect to the koi pond, Peter will prevail.

(B) Even though Peter owed Stewie a duty of reasonable care with respect to the koi pond, Peter's construction of the fence probably satisfied that duty.

(C) Because the koi pond was visible from the sidewalk, Stewie will prevail.

(D) Because Stewie did not appreciate the danger posed by the koi pond, Stewie will prevail.

Quint picked up Horton on his way to the park, where they planned to play basketball. On the way, Quint stopped concentrating on the road ahead of him and collided with a car driven by Yancey, who had stopped at a red light. Quint panicked and ran from the scene without helping Horton, who suffered a head injury in the collision. Yancey was uninjured but also failed to help Horton. Horton's injuries were exacerbated by the delay in receiving medical treatment.

40. If Horton sues Yancey, which of the following statements is most likely correct?

(A) Because Yancey was blameless in the accident, Horton will lose.

(B) Because any duty on Yancey's part to assist Horton was secondary to a duty owed by Quint, Yancey cannot be held liable.

(C) Because Yancey failed to assist Horton, Yancey will be liable for any injuries Horton received as a result of the delay in receiving treatment.

(D) Because Yancey failed to assist Horton, Yancey will be liable for all of Horton's injuries.

One Sunday, Hank was home with his son Bobby, age 10. Hank's wife Peggy was at work. Bobby was bored, so Hank decided to take them to Arlene's, a hardware store, where he planned to shop for a new drill. While Hank was looking over the selection of drills, Bobby wandered away into the power saw aisle. Bobby was touching a power saw hanging on a hook when the hook gave way and the saw fell, its blade cutting Bobby's arm. As it happens, the hook was loose. Bobby sues Arlene's for negligence. Assume the jurisdiction follows the common law rules about entrants to land. Arlene's moves for summary judgment based on these facts.

41. Which of the following statements is correct?

(A) Because Bobby was not in Arlene's for the purpose of purchasing anything, he will be classified as a trespasser. Because Arlene's only owed Bobby a duty to refrain from willful and wanton misconduct, and it is clear that no such conduct occurred, the court will grant Arlene's motion for summary judgment.

(B) Even though Bobby was not in Arlene's to purchase anything, he will be classified as an invitee to whom the store owes a duty of reasonable care. The court will deny Arlene's motion for summary judgment.

(C) Bobby's status in Arlene's was that of a licensee. Because Arlene's only owed Bobby a duty to warn of hidden dangers of which it was aware, and because there is no evidence that Arlene's knew the hook was loose, the court will grant Arlene's motion for summary judgment.

(D) Regardless of Bobby's status, the court will grant Arlene's motion for summary judgment because Hank's negligence in allowing Bobby to wander away superseded any potential liability of Arlene's.

On a commercial airline flight, things were going fine until the captain accidentally played for the passengers a pre-recorded announcement stating that the plane was about to crash into the sea. There was no actual emergency, and after a short time, the captain realized the mistake and announced that all was well and that the first announcement had been a mistake. Daphne, an elderly passenger, suffered a serious anxiety attack as a result of the erroneous announcement. A physician was on the plane, but failed to take any steps to help her.

42. If Daphne sues the physician for negligence, which of the following statements is most likely correct?

(A) Because the physician had the ability to assist, his failure to do so constituted actionable negligence.

(B) Because all the passengers were in a special relationship with each other, those with medical expertise had a duty to assist. The physician's failure to assist constituted actionable negligence.

(C) Because the passengers were in a special relationship with each other, those with medical expertise had a duty to assist. If, by assisting, the physician could have prevented some of the harm Daphne suffered, his failure to assist constituted actionable negligence.

(D) The physician will not be held liable for failing to assist.

Officer Krumpke went to Willie's home to investigate a claim that Willie had broken into a residence. When the person who answered the door called for Willie, Willie came downstairs. As soon as he saw the uniformed officer, however, Willie ran back up the stairs. Krumpke could tell that the stairway was dangerous because of rotting wood, but pursued Willie, trying to avoid the worst spots. Unfortunately, Krumpke fell through one of the stairs and sustained a serious injury.

43. If Krumpke sues Willie for negligence, which of the following statements is most accurate?

(A) Because Officer Krumpke was at Willie's home on police business and suffered an injury as a result of Willie's negligent maintenance of the stairway, Krumpke will recover.

(B) Because Officer Krumpke suffered an injury at Willie's home while conducting police business, he will not recover.

(C) Because Willie did not have an opportunity to warn Officer Krumpke of the dangerous condition of the stairs, Willie did not breach a duty of care, and Officer Krumpke cannot recover.

(D) Because Officer Krumpke failed to exercise reasonable care for his own safety, his recovery will be reduced.

44. Suppose negligence law were to impose a general duty to exercise reasonable care to avoid causing harm, through both affirmative conduct and failure to act. Why might it be unwise to impose this general duty, eliminating what are now sometimes called "no-duty rules"?

ANSWER:

A driver negligently crashes her vehicle into one driven by a woman who is 32 weeks pregnant. The pregnant woman is slightly injured and the fetus suffers a more severe head injury. The fetus continues to develop and emerges into the world as a relatively healthy infant. Its parents wish to bring a lawsuit on behalf of the infant against the driver. Assume that the jurisdiction permits abortions for any reason through 36 weeks of pregnancy.

45.　　If the parents sue, what argument about no duty could the driver raise, and why would it fail?

ANSWER:

On a dark night, Rebecca was driving north on a narrow road in suburban Ford City. Because there were no streetlights and no cars were approaching, Rebecca clicked on her high beams and drove for a mile or two without encountering another car. When a southbound car driven by Norm approached, Rebecca did not dim her headlights. A few moments after the cars passed each other, Norm struck a moose that had wandered onto the road. The moose was owned by Carla, who kept it in her yard nearby. The yard was surrounded by a fence, but a few minutes earlier, the moose had broken through the fence and escaped when it was frightened by the sound of a low-flying jet. Norm's car was badly damaged in the collision, and the moose was killed.

46.   Assume for purposes of this question that Rebecca is found liable to Norm for negligence. Carla sues Rebecca for negligence, seeking damages for the death of her moose. Which of the following statements is most likely correct?

(A)   Because keeping the moose was a dangerous activity, Carla should not recover for Rebecca's negligence.

(B)   Because Rebecca has already been forced to pay Norm damages resulting from the collision between his car and the moose, holding Rebecca liable to Carla would constitute improper imposition of double liability for the same accident.

(C)   Because an animal wandering into the road ahead was not a foreseeable victim of Rebecca's negligence in failing to dim her headlights for Norm's approaching car, Rebecca should not be held liable.

(D)   Rebecca should be held liable.

Bacteria in the water supply of Cropher City caused many people, including Seneca, to become ill. Seneca sues Cropher City for negligence. Assume Cropher City is not immune. Assume Seneca offers the evidence just stated and asks the court to employ the doctrine of res ipsa loquitur.

47.   Which of the following statements is most accurate?

(A)   The court should employ the doctrine because the water probably would not have become contaminated in the absence of negligence.

(B)   The court should employ the doctrine because drinking water normally does not become contaminated when reasonable care is used.

(C)   The court should employ the doctrine because any contamination of the water supply probably occurred when the water was under the control of the city.

(D) On these facts, the court should not employ the doctrine.

48.   A minority of jurisdictions hold that a defendant's violation of a relevant statute is not negligence per se, but merely evidence of negligence. Explain how this minority approach differs from the majority "negligence per se" approach.

ANSWER: *Minority view allows for imposition of negligence per se but not when state violated in exercise of due care.*

For more than ten years, Maurice had been involuntarily committed to a private psychiatric hospital (Hospital). Maurice suffers from pyromania (a tendency to set fires), and he has remained committed because Hospital personnel believe he still presents a danger of harm to himself or others. Recently, however, Hospital approved Maurice's request to take a weekend furlough in Mexico. While on the furlough, Maurice set fire to his hotel mattress. The fire damaged the room, and Mexican authorities arrested him and charged him with arson. While in jail awaiting trial, Maurice was attacked and injured by other jail inmates. After Maurice returned to the United States, his guardian filed a negligence action against Hospital, alleging that its decision to allow him to take the furlough was unreasonable. The complaint seeks compensation for the injuries Maurice suffered in the attack.

Hospital denies it acted negligently in approving Maurice's furlough. At trial, it offers evidence that weekend furloughs can be beneficial in the treatment of mental patients.

49.   If the jurisdiction treats customary conduct by members of the healing arts in the same fashion as customary conduct by people in other industries, which of the following statements concerning this evidence is most likely correct?

(A) If mental patients' recoveries would be impeded if they were not allowed to have such furloughs, it is less likely Hospital will be found negligent.

(B) If it is customary to approve furloughs of this kind, Hospital cannot be found negligent.

(C) If mental patients' recoveries would be impeded if they were not allowed to have such furloughs, it is less likely Hospital's action was a cause in fact of Maurice's harm.

(D) The evidence will have no effect on the case.

Cab driver Jerry was in a hurry to drop off his passenger so he could pick up his next customer. Jerry maneuvered his cab through busy downtown River City until he approached George's destination. As they neared the address, George, his passenger, said, "here's my building." Jerry switched from the left lane to the broad right lane, and stopped just before an intersection, about ten feet from the curb. George paid the fare and stepped out of the cab, directly into the path of a car driven by Elaine, who had just robbed a bank and was fleeing at high speed. George did not see Elaine's car coming and was not contributorily negligent.

A statute makes it unlawful for a cab or bus to drop a passenger off more than six feet from a curb. The statute was enacted to protect passengers' safety and to prevent cabs and buses from tying up traffic. Violation carries a $50 fine.

50. George sues Jerry for negligence, basing the duty on the statutory standard. If Jerry claims he should not be responsible for the accident, which of the following best represents the court's most likely response?

(A) Because the harm to George came about by a type of risk from which the statute was designed to protect him, George will prevail.

(B) Because George was immediately harmed by a party not within Jerry's control, Jerry cannot be held liable.

(C) Because the harm would have occurred regardless of Jerry's conduct, Jerry cannot be held liable.

(D) Because the harm came about as a result of the conduct of a criminal intervening actor, Jerry cannot be held liable.

Same facts as in Question 50. Suppose that for many years, about half the city's cabs and buses have often violated the statute.

51. If George sues Jerry for negligence, and Jerry wishes to make use of the fact that violation of the statute is common, which of the following best represents the court's most likely response?

(A) Though custom is relevant on the question of reasonable care, it is never the sole measure. The jury may consider the custom when deciding whether Jerry breached a duty of reasonable care toward George, but it may not consider the custom as the sole evidence of reasonable care.

(B) Because the legislature must have enacted the statute knowing of the custom, the jury may consider the custom when determining whether Jerry's violation of the statute was reasonable under the circumstances.

(C) Because Jerry's conduct was similar to that of the great mass of bus and cab drivers, he was not negligent.

(D) The customary conduct of many cab and bus drivers will not excuse Jerry's violation of the statute.

One Saturday, Danny took his daughter Angela, age six, to an amusement park owned by AmuseCo to ride the carousel. Angela climbed onto one of the horses, and Danny attached the little safety belt around her waist. He then stood at the side of the horse to hold Angela in case she needed help. The music started, the carousel began to turn slowly. Instead of settling in at a constant rate of speed, the carousel continued accelerating. Angela was thrown from her horse onto the spinning platform, breaking her leg. Angela sues AmuseCo for negligence. At trial, she offers in evidence the facts just stated, and then rests. AmuseCo moves for a directed verdict on the ground that Angela has not offered any evidence of negligence. Angela responds that the court should deny the motion because of the doctrine of res ipsa loquitur.

52.   Which of the following statements is most likely correct?

(A) Even if res ipsa loquitur applies, it can only be used to supplement other direct evidence pointing to negligence on defendant's part. Here, because no such evidence was offered, the court should grant AmuseCo's motion.

(B) While it is possible that res ipsa loquitur can be applied, expert testimony is always required when the issue concerns whether a malfunction in a mechanical device was caused by negligence. Because Angela has not offered such evidence, the court should grant AmuseCo's motion.

(C) Because possibilities other than negligence can explain the accident, the doctrine does not apply, and the court should grant AmuseCo's motion.

(D) Because the circumstantial evidence supports the inferences necessary for application of res ipsa loquitur, the court would not err in denying AmuseCo's motion.

Same facts as in Question 52. Assume that, correctly or incorrectly, the court denies AmuseCo's motion for directed verdict. AmuseCo offers no evidence to support its contention that it was not negligent in operating or maintaining the carousel. Assume the jurisdiction in which the action is filed does not hold that the res ipsa loquitur doctrine creates a "presumption" of negligence. Angela now moves for a directed verdict on the issue of negligence.

53.   Which of the following statements is most likely correct?

(A) Because AmuseCo failed to offer evidence of non-negligence, the court should grant Angela's motion.

(B) Because the inference of negligence is so strong under the circumstances, the court should grant Angela's motion.

(C) Because there is a jury question on the issue of negligence, the court should deny Angela's motion.

(D) Because AmuseCo has better access to information concerning the cause of the accident, the court should grant Angela's motion unless AmuseCo agrees to present evidence showing how the accident occurred.

Same facts as in Question 52. Assume that instead of declining to offer any evidence of non-negligence, AmuseCo calls a witness who testifies that, just before Angela got on the carousel, he saw someone tinker with the carousel's apparatus and then run away. Both parties then move for a directed verdict on the issue of negligence.

54.   Which of the following best represents the court's most likely response?

(A)   Because AmuseCo was not negligent, the court should grant its motion for directed verdict. The court should deny Angela's motion.

(B)   Because AmuseCo was negligent, the court should grant Angela's motion for directed verdict. The court should deny AmuseCo's motion.

(C)   Because any verdict by the jury would be based solely on speculation, the court should require the parties to offer additional evidence on the issue of negligence.

(D)   Because there is evidence to support either position on the question of negligence, the court should deny both motions.

Sam and Rebecca, both 10, were playing tag in the park. At one point, Sam lunged toward Rebecca to tag her. He missed and instead hit Lily, a jogger who was running past at the time. Lily fell to the ground, injuring her knee. Lily sues Sam for negligence to recover for her knee injury.

55.   Which of the following statements is most likely correct?

(A)   Because Sam was a young child, he cannot be liable for negligence.

(B)   Because Sam was a child engaged in the kind of activity normally associated with children, he did not owe Lily a duty to act reasonably.

(C)   Because Sam was a child engaged in the kind of activity normally associated with children, the jury will be allowed to consider his age when determining whether he breached his duty of reasonable care toward Lily.

(D)   Because Sam was engaged in a dangerous game, he was required to exercise the same degree of care as a reasonably prudent adult.

56.   In a lawsuit, the plaintiff claims that the defendant was negligent. The defendant was voluntarily intoxicated while she engaged in the conduct at issue. On what basis should the jury take into account the defendant's intoxication?

(A)   The jury should hold the defendant to the standard of a reasonable intoxicated person.

(B)   The jury should hold the defendant to the standard of a reasonable sober person.

(C)   The jury should hold the defendant to the standard of a reasonable person with a mental deficiency.

(D)   None of the above. The defendant is negligent as a matter of law.

In the famous case of United States v. Carroll Towing, Judge Learned Hand spoke of three variables: (1) the probability of a bad outcome occurring, or P, (2) the severity of the outcome that would result, or L, and (3) "the burden of adequate precautions," or B. The events of Carroll Towing took place in New York harbor during World War II. The alleged negligence at issue was failure to have a person on board working as a barge attendant, and the injury was harm to a ship.

57.   If similar events had taken place in a quiet, idle harbor during peacetime, how might Carroll Towing's totals for P, L, and B compare to the quiet hypothetical alternative?

(A)   *P* and *L* would go up, but *B* would go down.

(B)   *P* and *B* would go up, but *L* would go down.

(C)   *P, L*, and *B* would all go up.

(D)   *P, L*, and *B* would all go down.

Golem was driving near a park. Though the speed limit was 25 mph, he was going 45 mph. Just after he rounded a corner, a child named Ronnie, who had been playing in the park, fell into the street. Golem did not see Ronnie in time to stop, and struck her. Ronnie sues Golem for negligence. Had Golem been traveling 25 mph or less, he would have been able to stop in time. The jurisdiction has adopted the doctrine of "negligence per se" in its most traditional, established form.

58.   Which of the following statements is most accurate?

(A)   Because Golem violated a statute designed to protect a class of persons including Ronnie from the kind of harm that occurred in this case, Golem was negligent.

(B)   Because Golem's violation of the statute is not sufficiently connected with the injury that occurred, Golem's violation of the statute does not make him negligent.

(C)   Because Golem violated a statute designed to protect a class of persons including Ronnie from the kind of harm that occurred in this case, the jury will be permitted to take into account his violation in determining whether he breached his duty of care.

(D)   Because safety is probably only one purpose of the speed limit statute, the statute cannot form the basis of the duty of care.

59.   What is the general standard of care for a physician in the practice of medicine?
ANSWER:

60.   When a child is a defendant in a negligence action, to what standard of care is the child held?
ANSWER:

When Yarble was operating his motorboat at a dangerously fast speed, he found himself about to collide with another motorboat, operated by Mizuoko. Yarble did not have enough time to stop and his motorboat collided with Mizuoko's boat. Mizuoko brought an action against Yarble for personal injuries. Yarble argued that, under the emergency doctrine, he did not have enough time to prevent the collision, and so should not be liable.

61.   Explain why Yarble's argument should fail.
ANSWER:

A car driven by Dave negligently struck Adam as Adam crossed the street. A few minutes later, a bystander took Adam to the hospital. The emergency room doctor who treated Adam negligently failed to notice Adam's serious head injury. A reasonable physician would have taken x-rays of Adam's head, and these x-rays would have revealed a serious concussion that required hospitalization. Instead, the doctor just cleaned and bandaged a less serious cut on Adam's leg, then released him from the hospital. Because of the doctor's failure to treat Adam properly, he suffered more harm from the concussion than he would have suffered if treated properly.

62. If Adam sues Dave for negligence, and Dave claims he should only be responsible for the amount of harm Adam would have suffered if properly treated in the hospital, which of the following statements is most likely correct?

    (A) In a jurisdiction adhering to a "directness" or "intervening cause" approach to proximate cause, the doctor's conduct will likely be deemed to have broken the chain of causation, absolving Dave of responsibility.

    (B) In a jurisdiction adhering to a "directness" or "intervening cause" approach to proximate cause, the doctor's conduct will likely not be deemed to have broken the chain of causation. Thus, Dave will probably be responsible for the additional injury Adam suffered.

    (C) In a jurisdiction adhering to a "scope of risk" or "scope of duty" approach to proximate cause, Adam's additional harm will likely be deemed outside the scope of risk created by Dave's negligence, absolving Dave of responsibility.

    (D) Because Dave had no control over the doctor's conduct, Dave cannot be responsible for any harm caused by the doctor's negligent treatment.

Fran was riding her bike one morning when a large open-bed truck, owned and driven by Robbie, passed her. Robbie had filled the bed unreasonably high with old newspapers that he was taking to the recycling center. A mild gust of wind hit the truck and caused a small stack of papers to fly out of the bed. One of these struck Fran in the face. She lost her balance and fell, sustaining injury. Fran sues Robbie for negligence.

63. Which of the following statements is most accurate?

    (A) Because the accident was caused by an intervening force of nature, Robbie will not be held liable in a jurisdiction adhering to a "directness" or "intervening cause" theory for determining the extent of liability.

    (B) Because the accident would not have happened had Fran not struck Earl, Robbie will not be held liable.

    (C) Even though a force of nature caused the newspapers to blow off the truck, Robbie will be held liable.

    (D) Because this event was not the culmination of a risk reasonably to be perceived from Robbie's conduct, Robbie will not be liable under a "scope of risk" theory.

64.   In what sense is "alternative liability" (as applied in the case of Summers v. Tice, 33 Cal. 2d 80, 199 P.2d 1 (Ca. 1948) (and other cases) contrary to standard principles of causation in tort law?

ANSWER:

Hannah suffered a heart attack. Her husband Hardy dialed 911, but was unable to get through because the phone lines were jammed with callers trying to obtain tickets for an upcoming concert by a very popular group, which had just become available. Unfortunately, Hannah died. Hardy has sued Phone Co. for negligence.

65.   If Phone Co. claims that there was no cause in fact relationship between its conduct and Hannah's death, which of the following statements is most likely correct?

    (A) Unless Hardy can prove that had the phone lines been open, Hannah would not have died, or that her life would have been extended in some meaningful way, Hardy will not prevail.

    (B) Unless Phone Co. can prove that had the phone lines been open, Hannah would have died anyway, or that her life would not have been extended in some meaningful way, Hardy will prevail.

    (C) If it was not foreseeable that the phone lines would be jammed and that a person would die because the 911 service would be unreachable, there was no cause in fact relationship between Phone Co.'s conduct and Hannah's death, and Hardy will not prevail.

    (D) Because Phone Co. did not act, there is no cause in fact relationship, and Hardy will not prevail.

In Rice v. Paladin Enterprises, Inc., 128 F.3d 233 (4th Cir. 1997), the court rejected Paladin's First Amendment challenge to a wrongful death action brought by the relatives and representatives of three people killed by a "hit man" who had read "Hit Man: A Technical Manual for Independent Contractors," which Paladin published. The killer followed the book's detailed instructions for conducting a "hit," and murdered Mildred Horn, her eight-year-old quadriplegic son Trevor, and Trevor's nurse by shooting the adults through the eyes and strangling the child. The "hit man" was hired by Horn's ex-husband, who wanted the $2 million his son had received in settlement for the injuries that caused his permanent paralysis. Assume plaintiffs sue Paladin for negligence.

66.   If the jurisdiction in which the action is brought follows a "directness" approach to proximate cause, which of the following statements is the court most likely to make?

   (A)   Because the "hit man" was an intervening criminal actor, his conduct breaks the chain of causation, and Paladin cannot be held liable.

   (B)   Because Paladin did not have any control over the "hit man," and had no way to know who might be harmed, Paladin cannot be held liable.

   (C)   Because it is unreasonable to predict that a person will commit acts of criminal violence after reading a book, Paladin cannot be held liable.

   (D)   Because the chain of events between Paladin's publication of the book and the shootings was unbroken, Paladin may be held liable.

A car driven negligently by Dan repeatedly struck Paula's car, causing damage and personal injury. Because she believed Dan would assault her, Paula did not get out of her car to exchange information, and drove away from the scene. When a passerby saw Paula leave the scene, she reported Paula's license number to the police, and Paula was arrested and charged with hit-and-run driving. Fortunately, she was acquitted at trial. Paula now sues Dan, seeking, among other things, damages for emotional distress suffered as a result of her arrest and prosecution.

67.   If Dan claims his conduct was not a cause in fact of the damages resulting from Paula's arrest and prosecution, which of the following statements is accurate?

   (A)   Unless Dan could have foreseen Paula's arrest and prosecution, Dan's conduct was not a cause in fact.

   (B)   Because Paula would not have been arrested but for Dan's conduct, Paula was a cause in fact of the arrest and prosecution.

   (C)   Because Paula would not be able to "prove the negative" (what would have happened but for Dan's conduct), the conduct was not a cause in fact.

   (D)   Because more than one factor contributed to Paula's arrest and prosecution, Dan's conduct was not a cause in fact.

68. Courts sometimes describe a particular antecedent occurrence as "sufficient" to have caused harm, but not "necessary." Does such an antecedent occurrence fulfill the but-for test of causation? Explain.

ANSWER:

Paul thought he might have a heart problem, and went to the emergency room. There, Doc mistakenly diagnosed Paul as suffering from fatigue, and sent him home. Paul died that night. Doc's diagnosis was mistaken. Paul had suffered a massive heart attack. It is undisputed that, if Doc had diagnosed him correctly, Paul would have had about a 40% chance of surviving. Sending Paul home reduced his chance of survival to near zero.

69. Which of the following statements is correct?

   (A) In a jurisdiction adopting a traditional view of causation, Doc will be liable for Paul's death.

   (B) In a jurisdiction following a traditional view of causation, Doc will not be liable for Paul's death.

   (C) In a jurisdiction adopting a "lost chance of survival" theory, Doc will be liable for all damages resulting from Paul's death.

   (D) In either a traditional jurisdiction or one adopting a "lost chance of survival" theory, Doc will be liable for all damages resulting from Paul's death.

At 2:00 A.M., Dolores awoke to the sound of a window breaking and two people walking around the kitchen of her home. Dolores became frightened, and decided to escape by climbing out her bedroom window. She made it out the window and to the detached garage, started the car, and was preparing to gun it down the driveway when she noticed that the driveway was blocked by a car owned by Carl, a neighbor from down the street. Carl had carelessly parked in front of the driveway, and was at home asleep. Dolores got out of her car and tried to escape on foot, but the burglars had heard the sound of the car's engine and caught her. The burglars injured Dolores before leaving with some of her valuables. Dolores has sued Carl, the neighbor, for negligence.

70. If Carl asserts that his conduct was not a cause in fact of Dolores's injury, which of the following statements is most accurate?

   (A) Because Carl's carelessness played only a minor role in Dolores's injury, his conduct was not a cause in fact of Dolores's injury.

   (B) Unless it was reasonably foreseeable that blocking the driveway could lead to an injury to Dolores, Carl's conduct was not a cause in fact of Dolores's injury.

(C) Carl's conduct was not a cause in fact of Dolores's injury unless Dolores shows that she would have been able to escape had Carl not blocked her driveway.

(D) Carl's conduct will be deemed a cause in fact of Dolores's injury unless Carl can show that Dolores would not have been able to escape even if Carl had not blocked her driveway.

Same facts as in Question 70. Assume for purposes of this question that Carl's conduct was a cause in fact of Dolores's injury.

71. If Carl claims that he should not be held liable, and the jurisdiction follows a "directness" approach to the problem of proximate cause, which of the following statements is the court most likely to make?

(A) The risk reasonably to be perceived defines the duty to be obeyed, and because no risk of personal injury to Dolores could have been foreseen as a result of blocking her driveway, Carl is not liable.

(B) Because the harm was immediately brought about by an unforeseeable criminal act of a third party, Carl is not liable.

(C) Because Carl's conduct was the first link in a chain of events that led to Dolores's injury, Carl is liable for that injury.

(D) Because some harm could be foreseen from the act of blocking Dolores's driveway, Carl is liable for all harm that occurred.

Same facts as in Question 70. Assume for purposes of this question that Carl's conduct was a cause in fact of Dolores's injury.

72. If Carl claims that he should not be held liable, and the jurisdiction follows a "scope of risk" approach to the problem of proximate cause, which of the following statements is the court most likely to make?

(A) The risk reasonably to be perceived defines the duty to be obeyed, and because no risk of personal injury to Dolores could have been foreseen as a result of blocking her driveway, Carl is not liable.

(B) Because the chain of events leading to the harm was broken by an unforeseeable criminal act of a third party, Carl is not liable.

(C) Because Carl's conduct was the first link in a chain of events that led to Dolores's injury, Carl is liable for that injury.

(D) Because some harm could be foreseen from the act of blocking Dolores's driveway, Carl is liable for all harm that occurred.

Courts sometimes hold that a defendant is not liable despite having been negligent, on the ground that the defendant's negligence was superseded by subsequent wrongdoing by another person. They rule against the plaintiff on proximate cause grounds.

73. What type of subsequent wrongdoing most warrants such an outcome of non-liability? Give an example, being sure to mention both the initial negligence of the defendant and the subsequent wrongdoing of the other person.

ANSWER:

Fran was on an early morning bicycle ride along Flower Street, a tree-lined road that ran slightly uphill. Fran often rode this stretch hard to get the maximum exercise. When riding that way, she would keep her head down much of the time, only looking up every so often to check ahead of her for other cyclists, joggers, and parked cars. This is a common way for cyclists to ride. At one point, she looked up, and seeing no parked cars, bicycles, or joggers, lowered her head again. Less than 10 seconds later, Earl, a jogger, emerged from a side street and turned onto Flower Street about a hundred feet in front of Fran. Earl began running along the side of the street, a couple of feet from the curb. Fran was traveling much faster than Earl, and caught up to him in about 15 seconds. Fran never saw Earl, however, and Earl did not know Fran was coming from behind. Fran's bike struck Earl, causing him injury when he fell, and further injury when he was struck almost immediately by a car.

74.   Earl sues Fran for negligence. In response, Fran has asserted the doctrine of assumption of risk. Which of the following statements is most likely correct?

    (A) Because being struck by a cyclist is an inherent risk of jogging, Fran owed no duty of reasonable care toward Earl to take precautions to avoid that risk. Earl will therefore recover nothing.

    (B) Because being struck by a cyclist is an inherent risk of jogging, Fran owed no duty of reasonable care toward Earl to take precautions to avoid that risk. However, Fran has violated her duty not to act willfully or recklessly. Therefore, Fran will be fully liable for the harm she caused.

    (C) Even if Fran negligently struck Earl, Earl assumed the risk because being struck by a cyclist is an inherent risk of jogging. Earl's recovery will therefore be reduced by the degree to which Earl's assumption of risk overcomes Fran's negligence.

    (D) Earl did not assume the risk.

75.   Which of the following statements about assumption of risk is LEAST accurate?

    (A) It must be voluntary.

    (B) The majority of jurisdictions now regard it, in its implied form, as comparable to comparative negligence.

    (C) It must be manifested to the defendant.

    (D) The plaintiff must have understood the risk.

Herrle was a nurse's aide at a hospital that treated many Alzheimer's patients. Alzheimer's sufferers are often violent, and Herrle knew that her job involved working with violent, combative patients. Herrle also knew about past incidents in which patients attacked aides, but she and other aides received training in handling violent patients. Marshall was such a patient. On previous occasions, she had hit hospital employees, and her admitting diagnosis noted her aggressiveness and a high risk that she would cause injury. One day, Herrle saw that Marshall was being aggressive with another aide who was trying to move her from a chair into bed. Herrle entered the room to help because she was afraid Marshall would fall. While she was helping, Marshall hit Herrle several times on the head, causing serious injuries. Herrle sues Marshall's estate for negligence, and the estate raises the defense of comparative fault.

76.   Which of the following statements is most likely correct, assuming that the jurisdiction maintains a pure comparative fault system?

(A) If a reasonable person with Herrle's training in dealing with mentally ill patients would not have intervened, Herrle's recovery should be reduced by the doctrine of comparative fault.

(B) If a reasonable person without Herrle's training in dealing with mentally ill patients would not have intervened, Herrle's recovery should be reduced by the doctrine of comparative fault.

(C) Because it was unreasonable for Herrle to approach Marshall while she was combative, Herrle cannot recover against Marshall's estate.

(D) If no harm would have occurred had Herrle not approached Marshall, Herrle cannot recover against Marshall's estate.

While shopping in Irving's Grocery Store (Irving's), Lina approached a display of glass jars of jam. The jars were stacked from waist height to six or seven feet from the ground, and the rows were separated by corrugated cardboard. The display was unreasonably dangerous, being both too high and too precariously constructed. Lina decided to buy a few jars. Realizing that she needed to be careful in order not to knock over the display, Lina slowly began to pull the first jar out. Just before the jar was completely out, the display began to shake, and Lina stopped pulling out the jar. She was about to push it back into the stack when Robespierre, another shopper, accidentally bumped his cart into Lina. This caused her hand to jolt forward, and the entire display fell over. Both Lina and Robespierre were knocked down and suffered glass cuts. Lina sues Irving's for negligence in designing and constructing the display. Lina has also named Robespierre as a defendant.

77.   If Irving's claims Lina was comparatively negligent, and the jurisdiction maintains a rule of pure comparative fault, which of the following statements is accurate?

(A)   Because Lina was an invitee to whom Irving's owed a duty of protection, any carelessness on Lina's part will not reduce her recovery.

(B)   Because Lina recognized the danger of pulling out a jar from the stack, she cannot recover whether or not her action was unreasonable.

(C)   If Lina failed to use reasonable care for her own safety, and her conduct was a substantial factor in causing the display to fall, the jury may reduce her award.

(D)   If Lina failed to exercise reasonable care for her own safety, and her conduct was a substantial factor in causing the display to fall, Lina can only recover if her fault was less than that of Robespierre and Irving's.

78.   Same facts as in Question 77. If Irving's claims Lina assumed the risk of injury, and this is a "secondary" assumption of risk type of case, which of the following statements is accurate?

(A)   Lina will recover nothing only if the risk was inherent in the activity and Irving's was merely careless.

(B)   Lina will recover nothing only if the risk was inherent in the activity and Lina appreciated the risk and voluntarily decided to confront it.

(C)   Lina will recover nothing only if she appreciated the risk and voluntarily confronted it.

(D)   Lina's recovery will be reduced only if she appreciated the risk and voluntarily confronted it.

79.   Sometimes a defendant will argue that its behavior, identified by the plaintiff as a breach of duty, was fully compliant with a statute. The defendant will further argue that its compliance is a defense to the claim of negligence. How do courts treat this contention?

ANSWER:

Paul had never been horseback riding before, but he decided to try it after he began dating an avid equestrian. Paul drove to Ed's Stables (Ed's), which was near his apartment. He approached an employee, mentioned that he'd never ridden a horse before but said he was anxious to learn. The employee handed Paul a form titled "Release," and told Paul he'd have to sign it before he'd be allowed to ride. In part, the form stated:

I recognize that there are inherent risks in any horseback riding activity. I am also aware of the possible risks and dangers inherent in participating in such activities, including, but not limited to, possible injury or property damage from falling from my horse, collision with other riders, physical strain and injury due to unfamiliar or unexpected movements of the horse, biting or kicking by the horse, and allergic reaction to the horse, saddle and equipment, or vegetation and foliage encountered while riding.

In consideration of Ed's for making its facilities available to me for my use for horseback riding and activities related thereto, I hereby agree to and do hereby fully release Ed's and its agents and employees from any and all liability which they may have for injuries, death, or any other damages resulting from any injury which I may sustain while engaging in horseback riding and activities related thereto.

Paul skimmed the form quickly and signed it. He was then placed on a horse and began to ride. After two minutes, the horse suddenly took off at a full gallop and left the trail. She then raised up on her hind legs, throwing Paul onto a cactus. He was seriously injured. The horse had never thrown a rider before. Paul sues Ed's for negligence.

80.   If Ed's defends on the ground that Paul assumed the risk by signing the Release, which of the following statements is most likely correct?

(A)   Because the document constituted an adhesion contract, it is unenforceable.

(B)   Because the document did not specifically mention the risk of falling off the horse and landing on a cactus, it is unenforceable.

(C)   Because Ed's knew Paul was an inexperienced rider, the release is unenforceable.

(D)   The release is probably enforceable.

Clifford went to a hockey game between the hometown Mighty Chickens, which were owned by the Sidney Corp. (Sidney), and the Coyotes. His seat, which was only five rows off the ice, offered an excellent view even though it was in the area behind one of the goals. During the first period, a player hit a blazing shot toward the goal and, as often happens, the puck flew off the ice. The puck flew slightly left of the goal and struck the transparent barrier protecting the fans. Instead of bouncing off the barrier, the puck shattered it, sending sharp fragments flying. One fragment struck Clifford in the face and badly injured his eye. The barrier had been severely weakened from earlier collisions with pucks and players. Though the cracks in the barrier were not visible to fans, a reasonable inspection would have revealed that the barrier needed to be replaced. Sidney had not inspected the barrier.

81.   If Clifford sues Sidney for negligence, and Sidney claims Clifford assumed the risk, which of the following arguments constitutes Clifford's strongest response?

(A)   Though the risk of this type of accident is inherent in sitting so close to the ice at a hockey game, Sidney's conduct was reckless, thus denying Sidney the assumption of risk defense.

(B) Though being hit by a flying puck is an inherent risk of sitting so close to the ice, the risk of being hit by flying fragments of the barrier is not. Clifford's recovery should only be reduced slightly.

(C) Though being hit by a flying puck is an inherent risk of sitting so close to the ice, the risk of being hit by flying fragments of the barrier is not. Clifford should recover fully.

(D) Because Clifford voluntarily chose to attend the game, he may not recover.

82. Although most jurisdictions have replaced contributory negligence with comparative negligence, the continuing effect of contributory negligence has not entirely disappeared. Explain.

ANSWER:

83. What is the difference between "primary" and "secondary" implied assumption of risk?

ANSWER:

84. Courts have been more willing to recognize mental deficiency in the context of contributory negligence than they have been in the context of primary (defendant) negligence. Explain why this inconsistency might not be unfair.

ANSWER:

Owner was developing a piece of land, a task that required a significant amount of earth and rock removal. For that purpose, Owner engaged BlastCo, a company that specialized in construction-related blasting. One blast sent debris flying through the air. Some of it struck a nearby house owned by Peter, shaking the house sufficiently to knock some valuable pottery off shelves, breaking it. Peter was aware of the blasting operations but took no steps to protect his pottery. Peter sues Owner. Assume BlastCo is an independent contractor.

85.   Which of the following statements is correct?

(A) Owner is not liable.

(B) Owner will be liable only if BlastCo acted recklessly.

(C) Owner will be liable as long as BlastCo's conduct was negligent (or worse).

(D) Owner is liable.

Same facts as in Question 85. After one of BlastCo's blasts, Owner filled a huge dump truck with the debris. As the truck drove away on a public street, the weight of the truck and its load damaged some water pipes buried below the road, causing a flood in Paul's house. Paul sues Owner.

86.   Which of the following statements is correct?

(A) Owner will only be liable to Paul if it was negligent to drive such a heavy load on that street.

(B) Owner will be strictly liable to Paul because blasting, including the hauling work related to it, is an abnormally dangerous activity.

(C) Owner will be strictly liable to Paul because hauling a huge and heavy load of debris on a public road is an abnormally dangerous activity.

(D) Owner will not be liable if there was no prohibition of trucks over a certain weight on that road.

Same facts as in Question 85. Assume Owner is liable for any torts committed by BlastCo. One of BlastCo's blasts created a strong shockwave that blew down a rickety old barn on property owned by Porter.

87.   If Porter sues Owner, which of the following statements is correct?

(A) Owner will be liable only if BlastCo was negligent in setting off that particular blast.

(B) Owner will be strictly liable.

45

(C) Owner will not be liable because there was no trespass of debris onto Porter's property.

(D) Owner will not be liable because Porter assumed the risk by maintaining a rickety old barn on his property.

OilCo stored gasoline in huge storage tanks. The tanks were kept on platforms 30 feet above the ground. One of OilCo's full tanks fell over when defective steel used to build the platform could not sustain the weight of the tank. The tank crushed a car owned by Patty, which was parked along the curb on the street next to OilCo's property. Patty sues OilCo.

88.   Which of the following statements is correct?

(A) OilCo will be strictly liable to Patty.

(B) OilCo will be liable to Patty if this type of platform was not customary in the oil storage industry.

(C) OilCo will only be liable to Patty if its failure to discover the defect in the steel platform was the result of negligence on its OilCo's part.

(D) OilCo will not be liable if it did not build the platform.

GasCo was in the business of delivering gasoline to gas stations. For this purpose, GasCo used tanker trucks. An undetectable defect in the hitch mechanism caused the trailer on one of its trucks to disengage while the truck was traveling along a highway. The trailer overturned and spilled much of its load. Within a few moments, a spark caused by a passing car ignited the gasoline vapors, and a huge fire broke out. Popper, driving another car, was unable to avoid the fire, and suffered significant burns when his car became engulfed in flames. Popper sues GasCo.

89.   Make an argument that GasCo should be held strictly liable for Popper's damage.
ANSWER:

Oliver was an amateur physicist. His basement was full of equipment, much of it gathered from junkyards. Oliver's dream was to find a way to create nuclear fusion at room temperature, a feat that, if successful, could solve the world's energy problems. He obtained several gallons of D2O (heavy water), then set up a high-voltage electrical generator that would send a current through a large glass container filled with the D2O. He hoped this would cause fusion of atoms in a palladium lattice immersed in the container. Oliver planned to run the equipment several hours each night for about a month, and then to dismantle the apparatus and analyze the physical structure of the palladium bar. If it contained a larger than expected number of helium atoms, Oliver would know that he was on the right track. Oliver expected the apparatus to make an extremely loud banging noise, and it did. But he ran the experiment as planned.

Moe was Oliver's next-door neighbor to the east. The banging noises issuing from Oliver's electrical generator were plainly audible in Moe's house, and kept him awake at night. Moe sues Oliver for carrying on an abnormally dangerous activity.

90.   Which of the following statements is accurate?

(A) If the noise issuing from Oliver's electrical generator poses an unusually high probability of great harm, it is more likely Oliver will be found liable.

(B) If the noise could be prevented by the exercise of reasonable care, it is more likely that Oliver will be found liable.

(C) If high-voltage electrical generators are commonly used in this community, it is more likely that Oliver will be found liable.

(D) If Oliver has not caused a physical intrusion on Moe's property, Oliver may not be held liable.

Ari, an amateur chemist, was working on an experiment in his home's basement designed to extract energy from a combination of water and the element palladium. At one point, just after Ari carefully uncorked a glass beaker containing the water and palladium, the contents unexpectedly and inexplicably became unstable. Ari ran for cover, and the entire apparatus exploded moments later, blowing out a window and sending a cloud of toxic matter into the neighborhood. The matter was heavier than the surrounding air, and soon deposited in and around the home of Curly, a nearby neighbor. Over the next several weeks, Curly became quite ill. Soon, all of his hair fell out, he gained 75 pounds, and he began to talk in a falsetto.

91.   If Curly wants to sue Ari, which of the following legal claims best suits these facts?

(A) A private nuisance action.

(B) A strict liability action alleging that Ari is carrying on an abnormally dangerous activity.

(C) A negligence action alleging that Ari unreasonably permitted the container to explode.

(D) An action for trespass to land.

Ahmid was a sculptor who liked to work on big projects in his back yard shop in a residential subdivision. His specialty was fashioning three-dimensional "murals" on large concrete walls. Ahmid would first construct the thick concrete wall (the average size was about fifteen feet long and about ten feet high). Next, he would use chalk to sketch his designs on the wall. Finally, he would don a set of goggles and earplugs, start up his power tools, and begin to blast away at the smooth surface, creating within a matter of hours a monumental bas-relief sculpture.

One person's art is another person's headache. Rosa, an emergency room doctor, lived next door to Ahmid. Rosa's hours were somewhat erratic, and it was not unusual for her to be home until early afternoon and then to work a long shift at the hospital until late at night. When her schedule allowed, Rosa loved to sit on her back porch with a cup of decaf cappuccino and the morning paper, taking in the morning air. Doing so, however, was very difficult on days when Ahmid was creating his artwork. The noise from the power tools would be very loud, and concrete dust would fill the air for about a block around. After a while, Rosa found it impossible to spend time on her back porch, both because the noise bothered her and because she became concerned about the possible ill effects of ingesting concrete dust. She contacted a lawyer about the possibility of filing an action against Ahmid.

92.   If Rosa sues Ahmid for carrying on an abnormally dangerous activity, which of the following facts, if true, would impair her chances of recovering?

(A)   Ahmid can avoid spreading dust into the air by enclosing his work area.

(B)   Rosa can avoid the noise and dust by going inside when Ahmid is working.

(C)   Rosa can enclose her back porch for less money than it would cost Ahmid to enclose his work area.

(D)   Many other people in the neighborhood also suffered from the noise and dust as much as Rosa.

93.   If Rosa sues Ahmid for private nuisance, which of the following facts, if true, would impair her chances of recovering?

(A)   Ahmid can avoid spreading dust into the air by enclosing his work.

(B)   Rosa can avoid the noise and dust by going inside when Ahmid is working.

(C)   The harm to Rosa from the noise and dust exceed the harm that would be suffered by the average person.

(D)   Many other people in the neighborhood suffered from the noise and dust as much as Rosa.

As Pecan City grew, farmland on the eastern edge of the city was converted to other uses. Clavin Enterprises (CE) purchased a parcel of east side land and built a complex to serve as its headquarters and main plant. CE manufactured computer chips, and its plant employed several hundred workers. Like most chipmakers, CE used toxic chemicals in its manufacturing process. CE workers were carefully trained in the proper use and storage of the chemicals, and CE followed and often exceeded all of the industry's customary safety guidelines for the use of toxics. One day, a CE worker was using a forklift to move a drum of toxic chemicals. The worker's route took him close to the edge of CE's property. Due to factors of which CE had no reason to be aware, one of the hydraulic lifts holding up the drum snapped, and the drum rolled off the forklift, and crashed through the fence separating CE's property from that of Diane, a soybean farmer. The drum split open, and the chemicals spilled out. Diane was not present at the time. CE immediately sent a crew to Diane's land to clean up the toxic liquid, but much of the liquid had already seeped into the soil, contaminating Diane's ground water and killing many of the crops. In addition, the heavy equipment CE used in the clean-up destroyed some of Diane's crops, some of which would not have been harmed by the chemicals.

94. Diane sues CE for negligence, claiming its worker negligently handled the drum of chemicals. Which of the following statements is most accurate?

    (A) CE had a duty to handle the drum with reasonable care, and because harm occurred when it was handling the drum, CE will be liable.

    (B) Because CE was experienced in handling chemicals, it had a higher duty than a less experienced company, and its failure to handle the drum in a manner that would prevent an accidental spill will make it liable.

    (C) CE had a duty to handle the chemicals with reasonable care, but because its procedures met or exceeded the industry's standards, CE will not be liable.

    (D) Because CE had no reason to anticipate the breakdown of the hydraulic lift, it will not be liable even though its conduct led to significant harm.

Al owns a home next to the multi-story parking garage of Springfield Mall, owned and operated by the Peg Co. The parking structure is open at the sides, and it backs up to a narrow alley. Al's home is just across the alley. On days when Al works the late shift in the mall, he likes to sleep until noon. A recent rash of auto thefts has led the Peg Co. to install alarms on all twenty vehicles it uses for security at Springfield Mall. Almost every morning, one or more of the alarms activate when the vehicles are touched by mall patrons or when heavy delivery trucks lumber by. The alarms make extremely loud siren-like sounds until mall employees turn them off, which sometimes takes thirty minutes. This has caused Al to lose a great deal of sleep, and the Peg Co. has refused his requests to remove the alarm systems from the vehicles.

95. If Al sues the Peg Co. for nuisance, which of the following statements is most likely correct?

    (A) Because the noise from the car alarms harms the general public, the appropriate redress is through an action for public nuisance. Therefore, Al's action will fail.

    (B) Because the Peg Co. does not intentionally set off the alarms, Al's action will fail.

(C) Because the sound from the alarms poses an abnormally high danger to Al and others in the community, Al's action will succeed.

(D) If the jury finds that the noise substantially interferes with Al's sleep and that a reasonable person could prevent the alarms from going off so easily or could arrange to have the alarms shut off more quickly, Al's action will succeed.

MotorCo was developing a new type of automobile engine at its plant in Humdrum City. Although the fuel source being tested was more explosive than gasoline, the engine, if successful, could help end the nation's dependence on oil as a fuel source. One day, a test car that was supposed to remain stationary while the engine ran suddenly shifted into gear, and the driverless car lurched forward, broke through a barrier separating the plant from the public highway, and struck a car driven by Potter that was traveling along the highway. Potter sues MotorCo on a theory of strict liability. Assume the case was being decided by Justice Blackburn, who wrote one of the opinions in *Rylands v. Fletcher.*

96. Which of the following statements best approximates what Justice Blackburn would say?

(A) Traffic on the highways cannot be conducted without exposing those upon them to the inevitable risk of accident. In the absence of negligence, therefore, MotorCo cannot be held responsible to Potter.

(B) Because MotorCo carried on its business in a densely populated part of River City, it was engaging in what might be termed a non-natural, or inappropriate use of its land. Therefore, MotorCo is prima facie answerable for all the natural consequences of its activity.

(C) Trespass is the direct and immediate application of force to the person or property of the plaintiff. Because the occurrence which damaged Potter's vehicle did not occur as the direct result of any action on the part of MotorCo, Potter can recover, if at all, only upon a showing of negligence.

(D) Potter did not take upon himself any risk of harm from these dangerous activities, and if MotorCo's experimental cars are likely to do harm if they escape its land, Potter should recover even in the absence of negligence on MotorCo's part.

97. Same facts as in Question 96. Assume Potter's strict liability action against MotorCo is brought on an "abnormally dangerous activity" theory under *Restatement (Second) of Torts* §§ 519-520. Which of the following statements is most likely correct?

(A) Because MotorCo's activity caused harm to a person outside the property, MotorCo is strictly liable.

(B) If the social benefit that might be gained from MotorCo's efforts outweigh the risk created by the activity, MotorCo cannot be held strictly liable.

(C) Because the feature of the experimental car that made it dangerous was the explosiveness of the type of fuel being used, MotorCo cannot be held strictly liable.

(D) If MotorCo could have prevented the car from slipping into gear by the exercise of reasonable care, it is more likely that MotorCo will be held strictly liable.

98. The keeper of an animal known to be dangerous is generally held liable without fault for harms that the animal causes, when these harms relate to its dangerous propensities. Which situations present exceptions to this general rule?

ANSWER:

99. In what ways does the six-factor analysis for strict liability in *Restatement (Second) of Torts* § 520 resemble a negligence analysis?

ANSWER:

100. How do courts apply proximate cause to strict liability?

ANSWER:

Kyle's house and Eric's house backed up to each other, with a public alley in between. Kyle used the alley to access his garage. Eric did not have a garage and seldom used the alley. Eric was a slob. Rather than confine his trash to the city-supplied trash bin, he tossed his extra trash bags in the alley by his back fence, hoping the city would pick them up. It didn't, and the unsightly trash heap grew week after week, attracting countless flies and partly obstructing the alley, making it difficult for cars, including Kyle's to squeeze by without being scratched.

101. If Kyle sues Eric for private nuisance based on the partial blockage of the alley, which of the following arguments most strongly supports Eric's defense?

(A) Because we must live and let live, Kyle's action will fail.

(B) Eric's conduct, if a nuisance, is a public nuisance with which the public authorities alone may deal.

(C) Because the trash has not invaded or interfered with Kyle's property, Kyle's action will fail.

(D) Because Kyle's car was not scratched by the trash heap, Kyle's action will fail.

Darren owns First Step, a board and care facility for mental patients who have been confined in a state hospital but who have been deemed ready for a measure of independence. The twenty patients at First Step all have jobs during the day, but must return each evening by 6:00 and remain at First Step until 8:00 the next morning. First Step is located in a large converted house in a residential neighborhood, is licensed, and is not in violation of any zoning ordinances.

Recently, Samantha purchased the house next door to First Step. One window looks directly onto the First Step property, and from time to time, Samantha has seen First Step residents running around inside the building partly or fully naked, something she considers offensive.

102. If Samantha sues Darren for nuisance, which of the following provides the strongest defense for Darren?

(A) Because Samantha can avoid being offended by simply not looking, her action must not succeed.

(B) Because First Step was operating before Samantha moved in, Samantha assumed the risk.

(C) Because these activities at First Step do not create a substantial and unreasonable interference with the use and enjoyment of her property, her action must not succeed.

(D) Because of the public interest in maintaining facilities such as First Step, Darren is not maintaining a nuisance.

Rebecca was driving on a dark road, using her high beams. When a car driven by Cliff approached, Rebecca tried to flip the handle to dim the headlights, but due to a manufacturing defect in the handle, it broke off in her hand, and the high beams stayed on. Cliff was temporarily blinded, and as a result lost control of the car and went off the road. Diane, a passenger in Cliff's car, was badly injured in the accident. Rebecca purchased her car from a new car dealer several years previously.

103. If Diane wishes to sue the car manufacturer, which of the following theories would offer Diane the best chance of succeeding and would be easiest to prove?

(A) A negligence theory aided by the application of res ipsa loquitur.

(B) An express warranty theory.

(C) An action for strict liability in tort.

(D) Each of the above theories has an equally good chance of success.

104. Explain the concept of implied warranty of fitness for a particular purpose, as codified in UCC § 2-315.

ANSWER:

Despite studies showing that drivers using cell phones are much more likely to be involved in accidents than drivers who are not using cell phones, Pamela's luxury car, manufactured by Lexura, came equipped with a cell phone. One morning, while driving along a busy highway during rush hour and using her cell phone, Pamela failed to negotiate a curve and hit the guardrail. She suffered personal injury, and her car was damaged. Pamela has brought a product liability suit against Lexura, alleging that the car was defectively designed because it included a cell phone.

105. Which of the following statements is correct?

(A) Because Pamela was not involuntarily exposed to the cell phone, but chose to use it, Lexura cannot be held liable.

(B) If studies showing the dangers of cell phones were not published at the time Lexura designed the car, Lexura cannot be held liable.

(C) If Lexura made no representation that it was safe to use the cell phone while the car was in motion, Lexura cannot be held liable.

(D) Pamela will have a chance of recovery against Lexura if she can demonstrate that the benefits of the cell phone were outweighed by the dangers associated with it.

106. Same facts as in Question 105, except assume that Pamela's car also struck a car driven by Aviram. Assume also that Lexura would be liable to Pamela for defective design. If Aviram also seeks recovery against Lexura on the same products liability basis, which of the following statements is most accurate?

(A) Because he was not a purchaser or user of the defective car, Aviram may not recover.

(B) Because Aviram did not rely on Lexura to provide a safe car, Aviram may not recover.

(C) Aviram may recover for his personal injuries and for damage to his car.

(D) Aviram can recover for his personal injuries, but not for damage to his car, which is not recoverable in a tort-based products liability action.

107. What are the major criticisms of the "reasonable alternative design" requirement as provided in *Restatement (Third) of Torts: Products Liability*?
ANSWER:

Homer loved chocolate-chip muffins. One evening, after he and his date Marge finished dinner at the Hungry Heifer, the two visited Maggie's Desserts to pick up a dozen muffins. Marge paid (she insisted), and the two headed back to Marge's apartment to enjoy the muffins. Halfway through his sixth muffin, Homer started choking. He grabbed his throat, stood up, thrashed around, turned as blue as Marge's hair, and fell to the floor, hitting his head on the table as he fell. Marge raised Homer to his feet and applied the "Heimlich Maneuver," which dislodged a large rusty nail from Homer's throat. Homer's head was bleeding profusely, and Marge rushed him to the hospital. As it turns out, Maggie's does not make its own muffins, but purchases them in large packages from Bart's Bakery, a large commercial bakery.

108. Homer sues Maggie's for products liability. Which of the following facts, if proven, would hinder Homer's chances of prevailing?

(A) Marge, rather than Homer, was the purchaser of the muffins.

(B) Maggie's was not the manufacturer of the muffins.

(C) The nail was placed in the muffin by a disgruntled former employee of Maggie's who sneaked into the kitchen of Maggie's.

(D) Homer felt something sharp in the muffin before he placed it in his mouth.

109. Same facts as in Question 108. If Homer also sues Bart's (the bakery that actually made the muffins) for products liability, which of the following facts, if proven, would hinder Homer's chances of prevailing?

    (A) Marge, rather than Homer, was the purchaser of the muffins.

    (B) The nail would have been detected by a reasonable inspection conducted by Maggie's before selling the muffin.

    (C) The nail was placed in the muffin by a disgruntled former employee of Maggie's who sneaked into the kitchen of Maggie's.

    (D) Bart's did not sell the muffin to Marge.

Because their wheels form a single line, in-line skates work much like ice skates. In-line skates provide a fast, exciting ride, but they are also more dangerous than old-fashioned roller skates. The parents of six-year-old Joni bought her a pair of in-line skates manufactured by RollersInc. As soon as she received her skates, Joni ran to the top of a hill, put on the skates, and took off. It wasn't as easy as she expected it to be. Joni's ankles collapsed inward as she gained speed, and she fell hard, sustaining serious injuries. She sues RollersInc under the *Restatement (Third) of Torts (Products Liability)*.

110. Assuming RollersInc can prove any necessary facts, which of the following arguments would help RollersInc's defense?

    (A) If reasonable parents would have known the dangers posed by in-line skates to a six-year-old skater, Joni's recovery may be reduced.

    (B) Joni's conduct in skating down a hill on her first experience with in-line skates was unreasonable.

    (C) RollersInc intended the skates to be used only by children over ten.

    (D) In-line skates are more expensive than traditional rollerskates.

Sally, age ten, was an experienced in-line skater who wanted to be the fastest kid on the block. To achieve even greater speeds, but knowing that this would affect her skates' stability, she decided to replace the existing wheels on her skates with a different kind. The process was very difficult because RollersInc, the manufacturer of her skates, had welded the wheel brackets into place. Still, Sally managed to change the wheels. She could indeed skate faster with the new wheels, but after she'd been skating for about an hour, she lost control while at top speed and suffered a bad fall. Sally has sued RollersInc under the Restatement (Third) of Torts: (Products Liability).

111. Which of the following potential arguments by RollersInc is NOT viable?

    (A) RollersInc was not a cause in fact of Sally's injury.

(B) RollersInc was not the proximate cause of Sally's injury.

(C) Sally assumed the risk of her injury.

(D) The skates were not defective because Sally misused them in an unforeseeable manner.

Skatz, a manufacturer of in-line skates, has the best quality control procedures in the business. While other companies inspect each skate once, Skatz puts each skate through three inspections. This is costly for Skatz, and any additional costs would make the skates unprofitable. Despite these procedures, the left skate in a pair purchased by Gordon from a sporting goods store left the Skatz plant with a weak wheel mount. After Gordon had used the skates for a month, the left skate suddenly collapsed, causing him to fall and injure himself.

112. If Gordon sues Skatz for product liability under the *Restatement (Third) of Torts: (Products Liability)*, which of the following statements is most accurate?

(A) Because Gordon was injured by a product manufactured by Skatz that deviated from its intended design and caused his injury, Gordon can recover.

(B) Because Skatz cannot operate profitably with any quality control procedures beyond those it already uses, Skatz cannot be held liable.

(C) Because Skatz's quality control procedures exceeded even what would be considered reasonable care, Skatz cannot be held liable.

(D) Because Gordon could recover directly from the store from which he purchased the skates, he cannot hold Skatz liable.

Believing that rising auto prices made it very hard for low-income people to afford new cars, Corvair Motor Co. (CMC) decided to design and manufacture a cheaper alternative. Its Workerswagon barely complied with federal safety standards and was a very basic car carrying a base price of just under $4000. Shortly after the car's introduction, Marge bought one and drove it for two years before giving it to her friend's son Danny as a college graduation present.

Six months later, Danny negligently ran a red light and was struck from the side by a car traveling through the intersection from his left. Danny's car door was displaced inward in the crash and badly injured him. He contacted an attorney, who learned that the steel beams placed in the car's doors to protect occupants were thinner than those used by all other auto manufacturers and that the design made it easier for the car's door to be pushed into the occupant when the car was struck from the side. The attorney also learned that this design feature saved CMC $200 per car and that had CMC used any of the other designs then in use, Danny's injuries would have been substantially reduced.

113. Danny sues CMC. Based on the facts provided and reasonable inferences that may be drawn from those facts, which of the following arguments offers CMC the best chance of defeating Danny's action or substantially reducing his recovery?

(A) Consumers do not expect inexpensive cars to offer as much protection as expensive cars.

(B) CMC complied with all relevant federal safety standards.

(C) Danny was comparatively negligent.

(D) Danny assumed the risk.

114. Same facts as in Question 113. What is the effect on Danny's products liability claim of the fact that Danny was not the purchaser of the car?

(A) The fact will make it less likely that Danny will prevail.

(B) The fact will make it more likely that Danny will prevail.

(C) The fact will have no effect on Danny's possible recovery.

(D) Without more information, it is not possible to determine the effect of the fact on Danny's possible recovery.

115. Courts generally reject liability for failure to warn of a risk that was not known, and could not have been known, at the time of marketing. Nevertheless, some courts have held that post-sale duties can arise after the risks become known. To whom are these post-sale duties owed, and what should a manufacturer do to fulfill these duties?

ANSWER:

116. In a defamation action by Roberta against Brunhilde, which of the following points would NOT be central to Roberta's prima facie case against Brunhilde for defamation?

    (A) Brunhilde posted a story on her website falsely saying that Roberta had been convicted of embezzlement five years ago.

    (B) Roberta experienced severe emotional distress that she attributes to the publication of Brunhilde's false story on the website.

    (C) Roberta has suffered harm to her reputation that she attributes to the publication of Brunhilde's false story on the website.

    (D) Brunhilde's website, containing the false story about Roberta on its home page, is fully operative, and its history indicates that many visitors have clicked on the site.

Editor Edsel printed a story in a daily newspaper, the Succotash Times, that described state senator Burt Bumpkin as corrupt. The story relied on an extensive, tape-recorded interview with a grandfather figure of organized crime, Magoo, who recalled his illegal contributions to Bumpkin's election campaign in the last year. Everything in the story that described Bumpkin's corruption was conveyed in quotations attributed to Magoo. Investigation has now revealed that Magoo suffers from senile dementia and in the interview had confused Bumpkin with another politician, long dead, whom he had bribed in decades past. His reminiscences about Bumpkin were false.

117. Bumpkin brings an action against Edsel and the Succotash Times. Which of the following additional facts, if substantiated, would most strengthen Bumpkin's claim?

    (A) During the interview, Magoo frequently referred to Bumpkin by the wrong name and apparently had trouble finishing his sentences. —Mentally incompetent - should probably know he was wrong

    (B) While admitting that he is a public figure, Bumpkin has asserted his "right to privacy" when reporters were investigating rumors of his marital infidelity.

    (C) Edsel is a close friend of Bumpkin's archrival in the state senate, and actively desires the downfall of Bumpkin's career.

    (D) The Succotash Times employs fact-checkers and prints a "Corrections" notice in each day's edition.

59

118. Even though truth is a defense to defamation claims, it is possible for a plaintiff to bring a successful defamation claim against a defendant for having said something literally true, if the statement is implicitly false and defamatory. Give an example.

ANSWER:

Professional baseball pitcher Rooster McHew has long been suspected of resorting to "spitballs" — baseballs that a pitcher illicitly moistens with saliva — in violation of major league baseball rules. Although by tradition the rule has not been strictly enforced, a new commissioner has cracked down on pitchers, and now those who throw spitballs can lose their jobs. McHew has always denied the spitball rumors. At a recent game, news reporters gathered around old-timer Perry Gay, retired from baseball twenty years ago, and asked him what he thought of McHew's successes. Perry Gay is the most infamous retired spitball-thrower in baseball history. "I think he gets by with a little help from his friend," Gay replied to the question.

119. Can Gay's remark support a defamation action by Rooster McHew against Gay?

    (A) No, because McHew has consented to Gay's expression of opinion.

    (B) No, because Gay's words are innocuous and cannot harm McHew's reputation.

    (C) Yes, because a reasonable person would infer that Gay was referring to spitballs.

    (D) Yes, because the privilege to offer an opinion on a matter of public comment is not present under these facts.

Restatement (Second) of Torts § 559 gives a definition of a "defamatory statement" that the courts cite frequently: it is a communication that tends to lower the plaintiff in the esteem of the community, or deter people from associating with her. Almost any statement about a person can be "defamatory," however, in the sense that someone might find the statement disgraceful. For example, calling a high schooler "an A student" might hurt her reputation at some schools.

120. How do courts deal with this problem in their definition of "defamatory"?

ANSWER:

Channel 7 news, based in the town of Eureka, aired a segment called "Rooted in Slavery" that looked at institutions and individuals who had lived in Eureka as slaveholders and enslaved persons in the nineteenth century. "Rooted in Slavery" took a "Where are they now?" look at this history, interviewing several persons who are successors and descendants of these institutions and individuals. The program claimed that Paul Henry Shipley, who had been the mayor of Eureka from 1851-1855, had owned five slaves. This allegation was false. Shipley had never owned a single slave and had indeed participated in the abolitionist movement. His descendants, owners of Shipley Shipping, have suffered lost business because their customers now associate the enterprise with slavery. They wish to bring an action against Channel 7 news.

121. Under the common law of defamation such an action by the individual descendants would fail, because

    (A) the real party in interest is Shipley Shipping, and a corporation cannot be defamed.

    (B) the dead cannot be defamed.

    (C) the statute of limitations has run on the claim.

    (D) the First Amendment to the United States Constitution offers a limited privilege to Channel 7 news that covers the facts of this case.

122. In a debate over whether to abolish the doctrine of slander per se, which of the following rationales militates most strongly in favor of keeping it?

    (A) Certain common accusations have predictable effects, and it would burden plaintiffs unduly to have to gather evidence of reputational harm when they are defamed by these accusations.

    (B) Slander, unlike libel, compels a plaintiff to prove reputational harm.

    (C) Technological innovation has not fully blurred the distinction between oral and written communication.

    (D) It is relatively easy for a plaintiff to prove financial harm with respect to business activity, but unduly difficult to prove reputational harm with respect to his or her private life.

123. Who encounters more onerous obstacles to building her prima facie case for defamation: a public *figure* or a public *official*?

    (A) A public figure, because public figures typically have more power in the media than do public officials, and can protect themselves against defamation.

    (B) A public figure, because the consequences of public figures' being defamed are less severe.

    (C) A public official, because of the public interest in permitting criticism of government.

    (D) A public official, because public officials enjoy relative immunity from defamation liability as defendants.

124. According to the common law, is truth a complete defense to defamation?

    (A) Yes.

    (B) No: Liability remains when the publication of truthful material is unjustified.

    (C) No: Liability remains when the defendant is motivated by actual malice.

    (D) No: Liability remains for exceptional invasions of privacy.

Legislator Lawrie delivered an impassioned speech in the well of the state assembly attacking "the Wall Street of Main Street," shortly before the legislature voted on a large appropriation to businesses in the state. In the speech Lawrie faulted several business leaders of the state for their inadequate commitment to citizen well being. The speech included an accusation by Lawrie that local millionaire Hilton employed undocumented workers to clean and serve food at his chain of hotels. This accusation was false, and Hilton believes he suffered financial loss as a consequence. Furthermore, Hilton finds the accusation gratuitous because his hotel, like all hotels in the state, was not in line to receive any funding from the appropriation being debated, and Hilton has no other business interests in the state.

125. A defamation claim by Hilton against Lawrie is likely to

    (A) succeed, because Lawrie's remarks lacked a reasonable relation to the legislative endeavor at hand.

    (B) succeed, because Hilton is a public figure.

    (C) fail, because Lawrie's remarks need not pertain to the legislative endeavor at hand in order to be covered by the legislator's privilege to commit prima facie defamation.

    (D) fail, because of Lawrie's First Amendment privilege to engage in debate on a matter of public interest.

126. Which statement most accurately describes the limited privilege to make a defamatory statement in a judicial proceeding?

    (A) The statement must be reasonably related to the issues raised in the proceeding.

    (B) The statement must implicate a matter of common public concern.

    (C) The statement must be reasonably tailored to minimize foreseeable harm to the person referenced.

    (D) The statement must be made in a criminal proceeding; the privilege does not apply in civil cases.

127. For purposes of bringing a defamation claim, a "public figure" is in a weaker position than an ordinary private citizen. The category has a few nuances. Describe the public figure in its strong form and its "limited purpose" form.

ANSWER:

Guests of innkeeper Stewart Marther would be surprised to learn that inside the headboards of their antique king-sized beds are embedded recording devices. Marther, who has owned the inn for ten years, enjoys sitting at a console in the front office, tuning in to the private conversations of guests in the rooms. Once his devices picked up the words of a married man named Jeff. Marther heard Jeff confess to his wife, in response to her questioning, that he, Jeff, had had homosexual experiences before their marriage. Marther repeated this gossip to mutual acquaintances, causing injury to Jeff.

128. Can Marther be liable to Jeff?

    (A) No, because the information that Marther repeated was truthful.

    (B) No, because the inn belongs to Marther and Marther has a privilege to enter the rooms of his property.

    (C) Yes, because a reasonable person would find the disclosure of homosexual conduct repugnant.

    (D) Yes, because Jeff had a reasonable expectation of privacy in his room in the inn.

The model Cassandra Philandra, standing nearly six feet tall, weighs 150 pounds. Although she appears slender, she has earned significant praise in the media for being "sensible" and "reasonable" in her size, in contrast to other models deemed "too thin." Journalist Elmer uncovered a bit of dirt about the "sensible" Cassandra: ten years ago, as a teenager, Cassandra had weighed 105 pounds and was hospitalized for eating disorders. Cassandra has just learned that six months ago Elmer repeated this truthful story about her to a circle of journalists. No media announcements have emerged. Cassandra has asked you to advise her about a possible action against Elmer alleging invasion of privacy.

129. You should advise her that she is

    (A) likely to prevail, because the matter is not of legitimate public concern.

    (B) likely to prevail, because this disclosure is highly offensive to a reasonable person.

    (C) unlikely to prevail, because she is a public figure.

    (D) unlikely to prevail, because there has been no publication to the public at large.

130. Why does tort law bother with privacy — that is, what value does privacy serve, and why is tort law needed to achieve this value?

ANSWER:

One small city remembers well the case of John Septuagenarian, an old man who lived alone at the edge of town. A teenage girl arrived at the police station and claimed she had escaped from Septuagenarian's house, where she had been kept in a basement dungeon. She showed the police the house. When they entered, they found six other girls in the basement. Septuagenarian had kidnapped and sexually abused them. On the testimony of the girls, whose names were kept from the public, Septuagenarian was convicted and sent to prison, where he died six years later. The town still talks about the trial. Last week the local newspaper ran a story about television actress Gina Mulcahy, age 26. According to the news story, Mulcahy had been one of the "Dungeon Seven," one of Septuagenarian's victims. The story is true. The newspaper learned the information from civil court records; two years ago Mulcahy filed a quiet, low-profile civil suit against the estate of Septuagenarian, and received a (relatively small) settlement from his limited assets. Mulcahy is embarrassed and distressed by the newspaper story.

131. Which of the following statements best describes Mulcahy's possible claim against the newspaper?

   (A) Mulcahy has a strong claim for invasion of privacy, but a weak one for intentional infliction of emotional distress.

   (B) Mulcahy has a weak claim for invasion of privacy because the information that the newspaper revealed was a matter of public record.

   (C) Mulcahy has a strong claim for invasion of privacy because the news disclosed is not a matter of public significance.

   (D) Mulcahy has a weak claim for invasion of privacy, but a strong one for intentional infliction of emotional distress.

132. Suppose you are a state supreme court judge considering whether to abandon your state's recognition of a tort claim for invasion of privacy. Which of the following considerations is LEAST relevant to that project?

   (A) The availability of other remedies for wrongful conduct, such as trespass and deceit.

   (B) The distinction between true and false disclosures.

   (C) Individuals' interest in keeping their private lives to themselves.

   (D) The public interest in defining "newsworthiness" broadly.

Tarpala runs a "business intelligence" consulting business. Her work consists of attempting to learn her clients' competitors' trade secrets and other informational assets kept from the public. In May, posing as a United Way charities solicitor on behalf of a client named Marco, Tarpala gained entry to the factory floor of Gobble Inc., a manufacturer of children's toys, and surreptitiously took pictures of the top-secret Christmas line. Marco used this information for competitive advantage against Gobble, Inc.

133. In an action by Gobble, Inc. against Tarpala for invasion of privacy, Gobble Inc. should

(A) prevail, because Tarpala engaged in fraud.

(B) prevail, because Tarpala's entry to the factory floor was not privileged.

(C) not prevail, because a corporation cannot bring an action for invasion of privacy.

(D) not prevail even assuming Tarpala has fulfilled the elements of invasion of privacy, because Gobble cannot prove that Tarpala's actions caused its losses.

A Hollywood actress, Hilda-May, earns $30 million per movie. Despite her wealth and fame, not to mention a busy schedule, Hilda-May has time and leisure to consider suing some of the many people who offend her.

134. Which of these behaviors would give Hilda-May her strongest claim for "appropriation of the plaintiff's name or likeness"? Assume that Hilda-May has consented to none of them.

(A) A struggling entrepreneur uses the name and photo of Hilda-May on the packaging of his new line of squash rackets.

(B) A start-up entertainment magazine prints a photograph of Hilda-May storming away from her boyfriend in a restaurant, and captions it "Hilda-May Flying Low!"

(C) A starving novelist names one of his characters Hilda-May. The character, a waitress with ambitions to sell a screenplay she has written, is manipulative and dishonest.

(D) A disgruntled ex-lover of Hilda-May's gives a long interview to Infotainment Tonite, a television show, describing their defunct relationship in painful detail. He is not paid by Infotainment Tonite, but he uses his appearance on the show to promote his self-recorded music.

Law professor Benita Bevilaqua thought nobody was nearby while she and three friends, guests in her condominium, smoked marijuana using her elaborate water-cooled pipe. As luck would have it, however, the building's smoke alarm went off and the building was evacuated. A television news crew came to the scene, and Benita's friend Jordan was videotaped clutching the pipe. Jordan told all who would listen whose pipe it was and what it was used for. Benita suffered damages related to professional disgrace.

135. Her lawsuit against the television station for invasion of privacy should fail because

   (A) there was no intrusion.

   (B) she experienced no injury.

   (C) the television station is not the proper defendant.

   (D) the gathering and dissemination were not unreasonable.

Gothika, a famous recording artist, has consulted you about bringing an action against FanRagZine, a magazine that had been struggling for two years and was about to shut down for lack of cash when it stumbled on a news story about Gothika: she had entered drug rehabilitation and was becoming a born-again Christian. FanRagZine published many photographs of Gothika and ran several stories about her transformation, all without her consent. Gothika can prove that FanRagZine gained hundreds of thousands of dollars by exploiting her story. She seeks a share of these profits on a theory of "appropriation," the subcategory within invasion of privacy.

136. Why would her claim be unlikely to succeed? Advise her.
ANSWER:

Maureen agreed to undergo surgery performed by Dan. Dan was HIV-positive, but did not inform Maureen of this fact because he genuinely believed it to be a private matter that posed no risk to her. Dan carefully avoided cutting himself during surgery, and the surgery was successful. Six months after the surgery, however, Maureen learned of Dan's HIV status. She became extremely apprehensive, and took an HIV test which, fortunately, proved to be negative. Nevertheless, the anxiety she suffered was extremely severe, and led to significant weight loss and other physical illness. Maureen has consulted an attorney, who is considering filing a claim for intentional infliction of emotional distress on Maureen's behalf against Dan.

137. Which of the following arguments gives Dan the greatest chance of avoiding liability?

(A) Because Dan did not act maliciously, he did not satisfy the intent requirement, and Maureen cannot recover.

(B) Because Dan's conduct was not "extreme and outrageous," Maureen cannot recover.

(C) Because there was no contact between Dan's blood and Maureen's body, Maureen cannot recover.

(D) Because claims of severe emotional distress can be faked easily, Maureen cannot recover.

138. Under what conditions might it be proper for a court to hold a defendant liable for negligent infliction of emotional distress as experienced by a "hypersensitive" plaintiff — that is, when the defendant's behavior would not have caused a normal, ordinary person to suffer emotional distress?

ANSWER:

District Attorney Doyle was sick and tired of divorced persons who failed to make court-ordered child support payments. To crack down on these "deadbeat parents," Doyle constructed a large billboard in a prominent location. Each month, the billboard featured a photo of the "Deadbeat Parent of the Month," and a statement of how much the person owed for child support. For April, and as an April Fool's joke on her old friend Giles Crane, Doyle posted Crane's photo and a statement that he owed more than $20,000 in child support. When Crane learned of the poster, he suffered serious emotional distress, eventually leading to the breakup of his marriage. He became a shut-in, refusing to leave his luxury condo. He sues Doyle for intentional infliction of emotional distress. Assume Doyle is not immune from suit.

139. Which of the following statements is accurate?

(A) Crane will not prevail because Doyle did not intend to cause serious emotional distress.

(B) Crane will not prevail because Doyle did not act maliciously.

(C) Crane will not prevail because he did not suffer bodily harm.

(D) Crane will likely prevail.

On a commercial airline flight, things were going fine until the captain accidentally played for the passengers a pre-recorded announcement stating that the plane was about to crash into the sea. There was no actual emergency, and after a short time, the captain realized the error and announced that all was well and that the first announcement had been a mistake. Daphne, an elderly passenger, suffered a serious anxiety attack as a result of the erroneous announcement. Daphne sues the airline for intentional infliction of emotional distress.

140. Of the following, which constitutes the airline's strongest argument against liability?

(A) Daphne was extra sensitive.

(B) There was no intent.

(C) The conduct was not extreme and outrageous.

(D) Daphne did not suffer physical injury.

Park, an Asian-American, worked as a secretary for Smith at BigCorp, a large corporation. Over a period of several months, Smith repeatedly derided Park's ethnicity in front of other workers. He uttered crude, disparaging remarks about Asian-Americans, adopted a stereo-typed accent, and frequently assigned Park the most menial tasks. Smith thought he was being funny, and was helping to promote camaraderie among the staff. However, Park became very upset, and complained to Smith's supervisor. When the supervisor failed to do anything about Smith's behavior, Park quit her job and sued BigCorp for intentional infliction of emotional distress.

141. Which of the following statements is most accurate?

(A) BigCorp is not liable because Smith's actions were not within the scope of employment.

(B) Park cannot recover unless she suffered physical illness as a result of Smith's behavior.

(C) Park cannot recover because Smith was not trying to cause emotional distress.

(D) Park has a strong case for intentional infliction of emotional distress.

142. "Negligent infliction of emotional distress" includes a range of emotional consequences under one doctrinal label. What sort of injuries may be compensable?

ANSWER:

One afternoon, Derek entered the First National Bank, pulled a gun from his coat, fired into the air, and ordered everyone to lay face-down on the floor. He then told the manager to get up and empty all the cash drawers into a sack. The manager complied. As Derek ran out of the bank, he yelled, "If anyone calls the police in less than 10 minutes, I'll hunt down every one of you and kill you in your sleep!" Paul, one of the tellers, was so distressed by this event that he was unable to sleep for several weeks, lost 30 pounds, and began to obtain psychiatric care. A little more than a year later, Cosmo consults an attorney about suing Derek, who was caught and convicted of bank robbery. Assume the statute of limitations for assault has already expired, but that a separate statute of limitations for intentional infliction of emotional distress has not yet run.

143. Which of the following statements is correct?

    (A) Cosmo has a strong claim for intentional infliction of emotional distress.

    (B) Because the facts primarily give rise to an action for assault, and the assault statute has run, Cosmo's claim is barred.

    (C) Even though the statute of limitations on intentional infliction of emotional distress has not expired, Cosmo has no action for that tort because Derek's conduct was not directed specifically toward Cosmo.

    (D) Because Derek has already been convicted of bank robbery, Cosmo's claim is barred.

Parker and Dawn, both 7th graders, liked to kid around with each other. One day, as Parker was placing her lunch tray on the table and starting to sit down, Dawn pulled the chair out from under her. Parker noticed this too late, lost her balance trying to avoid falling, and spilled the entire tray of food onto her clothes. Dawn and the others at the table began to laugh loudly, and soon the entire cafeteria was looking at Parker and laughing. Parker began to cry and ran from the room to the school nurse, who called her parents to pick her up. For several weeks, Parker felt so humiliated that she refused to return to school. In addition, she became physically ill, stopped eating, and needed to be placed on medication to improve her appetite.

144. If Parker sues Dawn for intentional infliction of emotional distress, which of the following statements is accurate?

    (A) Parker's claim will probably fail because Dawn's behavior was not extreme and outrageous.

(B) Parker's claim will probably fail because Dawn did not mean to injure her.

(C) Parker's claim will probably fail because she assumed the risk.

(D) Parker has a strong claim.

Ronald was eating lunch with Paddy in the company cafeteria when Diego, another employee, solemnly approached him and said: "We just got a call from County General. Your wife has been admitted with severe injuries from a car accident. They don't think she's going to make it." Ronald ran from the room and headed for County General. On the way, his wife called to ask him to pick up some milk on the way home. She was fine; there had been no accident. Diego had played a prank on Ronald. Meanwhile, Paddy, who, unknown to Diego was a close friend of Ronald and his wife, suffered severe emotional distress. Though he learned later in the day that the whole thing was a prank, his anxiety was severe, and he required psychiatric care.

145. If Paddy sues Diego for intentional infliction of emotional distress, which of the following statements is correct?

(A) Paddy has a strong claim.

(B) Paddy will lose because Diego's conduct was not "extreme and outrageous."

(C) Paddy will lose because he did not suffer bodily harm.

(D) Paddy will lose because it was not reasonably foreseeable to one in Diego's position that Paddy would suffer severe emotional distress.

Peter, his wife Pauline, and their son Padua drove together to the Sparkle Car, a car wash. Sparkle Car was a drive-through place, and customers were permitted to remain in the car while it rolled through the washing and drying areas. Peter and Padua remained in the car, while Pauline got out, intending to watch the car through thick windows along the way. When the car was part way through, one of Sparkle Car's employees negligently handled a piece of equipment, causing it to crash through the passenger-side window and impale Padua. Peter was looking the other way when this happened, but Pauline saw the whole thing and immediately fainted from emotional distress. Peter also became extremely upset when he noticed what had happened a few moments later.

146. If Pauline sues Sparkle Car for negligent infliction of emotional distress, which of the following statements is correct?

(A) If the court applies the most common test, Pauline's case will fail.

(B) If the court applies the "impact" rule, Pauline will prevail.

(C) Regardless of the test used, Pauline's case will fail because Pauline was not in the zone of danger caused by the employee's negligence.

(D) Regardless of the test used, Pauline will prevail.

147. Same facts as in Question 146. Assume that when the piece of equipment broke the car window, flying glass also injured Peter, who was sitting in the driver's seat. If Peter wishes to sue Sparkle Car, and seeks to recover for his emotional distress at his son's horrible injury, which of the following statements is correct?

(A) Peter will not recover any damages because he did not witness the injury occurring to Padua.

(B) Peter will recover for his bodily injury, but will not recover for emotional distress if that kind of harm was not a reasonably foreseeable consequence of improperly handling the equipment.

(C) Peter will recover both for his bodily injury and for the emotional distress he suffered on observing his son's injuries.

(D) Peter will recover for his bodily injury, but whether he will recover his emotional distress damages depends on the test used in that jurisdiction for the tort of negligent infliction of emotional distress.

148. Same facts as in Questions 146, except assume that Peter was not physically injured in the accident. If Peter wishes to sue Sparkle Car for negligent infliction of emotional distress, which of the following statements is correct?

(A) Peter will not recover under either the "impact" or "zone of danger" rules.

(B) Peter will not recover under the "impact" rule, but will recover under the "zone of danger" rule.

(C) Because Peter did not witness his son's impaling, but only saw the consequences a few moments later, he may not recover under the more lenient test of cases such as Dillon v. Legg, but may recover under the "zone of danger" test.

(D) Peter will recover under any test for negligent infliction of emotional distress.

Perry was visiting her friend, who was in the hospital fighting an infection caused by AIDS. While Perry was standing by her friend's bed, a hospital nurse drew some blood from the friend's arm. After she drew the blood, the nurse negligently stuck Perry's arm with the needle. Perry contacted a doctor, who advised her that it would be six months before she would learn whether she had been infected. During that period, Perry suffered enormous anxiety and dread. Ultimately, she learned that she had not been infected. Nevertheless, Perry wishes to sue the hospital for negligence.

149. Discuss the likelihood that Perry will be able to recover.
ANSWER:

Glenda received a telegram one evening notifying her of the death of her father. This was entirely unexpected; her father had been in perfect health, and she had spoken to him just the day before. As it happens, the telegram was in error. Another person with the same name as Glenda's father had died, and the telegraph company had addressed the telegram to the wrong family. Glenda was extremely distraught, and it took her several days to find out that the telegram was in error. Over a period of several months, Glenda suffered loss of sleep, headaches, and constant stomach pain. She wishes to sue the hospital for negligent infliction of emotional distress.

150. Which of the following statements is correct?

(A) Because Glenda was not present when the telegram was incorrectly addressed, she cannot recover.

(B) Because Glenda was not physically endangered by the negligent act, she cannot recover.

(C) Because Glenda was extra sensitive, she cannot prevail.

(D) Glenda's claim has a reasonable chance of success.

Partners of the law firm of Hoof & Mouth knew that the managers of its corporate client, Regiment, were given to making false representations. When Regiment sought to apply for a loan from Metrobank, its managers gave Hoof & Mouth documentation about its ownership of various assets. The Hoof & Mouth partners knew that Regiment managers had written material false statements into this documentation. Nevertheless, they helped redraft the documentation to make it look more convincing, and submitted these papers in the loan application to Metrobank. Regiment later defaulted on the loan and it is now insolvent.

151. In a lawsuit by Metrobank against the Hoof & Mouth partners, Metrobank should prevail because

   (A) although the true wrongdoer is Regiment, as between Metrobank and Hoof & Mouth, Hoof & Mouth should bear this loss.

   (B) the Hoof & Mouth partners knowingly assisted in the commission of tortious fraud.

   (C) the Hoof & Mouth partners were the agents of Regiment.

   (D) the representation of Regiment was unlawful, and harms to Metrobank flowed proximately from this wrong.

152. Which of the following is NOT an element of the tort of intentional misrepresentation?

   (A) Knowledge of the consequences of falsity.

   (B) Knowledge that the statement made was false.

   (C) Intent to induce reliance.

   (D) Materiality of the statement.

Gargle, a celebrated bass-baritone singer, entered into an agreement with the Liberace Opera House to perform the title role in Mozart's "Don Giovanni" in September, one year after the contract was signed. Unfortunately, over Labor Day weekend, shortly before the scheduled opening night, Gargle's favorite bartender served him an expensive wine that, unknown to the bartender, had gone bad. Gargle ended up stricken with nausea and vomiting. The resulting harm to his voice caused Gargle to have to cancel his appearance, which in turn forced the Liberace Opera House to spend thousands of dollars refunding advance tickets. In addition, the Liberace Opera House had to hire a substitute singer and pay him a salary. The Liberace Opera House sues the errant bartender and her employer, Da Ponte Lounge.

153. The Liberace Opera House should

(A) prevail, because a reasonable bartender would have known not to serve the wine in question and Da Ponte Lounge is liable under respondeat superior.

(B) prevail, because the expenditures that Liberace Opera House spent in response to Gargle's harm were foreseeable.

(C) not prevail, because there is no tort liability for negligent interference with contractual relations.

(D) not prevail, because the contract between Gargle and Liberace Opera House encompassed this contingency.

In order to obtain financing to buy an ongoing business, Dolly asked her husband, Madison, to hire an accounting firm and have that firm prepare an audited statement of Dolly's and Madison's joint net worth. Unknown to Dolly, Madison was engaged in various ongoing frauds. Dolly thought she and Madison were worth about $10 million, but actually they had less than $1 million in assets. Madison produced for Dolly an "audited financial statement," actually a document prepared by a crony of his, which grossly overstated the couple's assets. Dolly appended this "audited financial statement" to her loan application. The lending bank scheduled an interview with Dolly in order to evaluate the loan application. An official of the bank asked Dolly whether she personally had chosen the accounting firm that prepared the financial statement. Dolly said yes. Some time later, Dolly and Madison defaulted on the loan. Assume the bank wants to sue Dolly (but not Madison).

154. Which claims would be plausible under these facts?

(A) Intentional misrepresentation only.

(B) Negligent misrepresentation only.

(C) Both intentional and negligent misrepresentation.

(D) Neither intentional nor negligent misrepresentation.

Louisa and Bonnie Blue were business partners who habitually made real estate purchases together. They submitted a written offer to purchase a country estate. This offer ran several pages long and was signed at the bottom by both Louisa and Bonnie Blue. Unknown to Bonnie Blue, Louisa removed the front page of the offer, the one that named and described the property, substituted a new front page describing a second property, and submitted this new document as an offer to a different seller, with both signatures at the bottom. Louisa was hoping, on behalf of herself and Bonnie Blue, to buy both properties quickly and sell them quickly. Louisa's tampering was discovered before the prospective sellers signed the contracts; both sellers decided that Louisa and Bonnie Blue were shady operators, and refused to deal with them. Consequently, the Louisa-and-Bonnie-Blue partnership lost money.

155. Which claims by Bonnie Blue against Louisa are plausible?

(A) Misrepresentation

(B) Tortious interference with contractual relations

(C) Both misrepresentation and tortious interference with contractual relations

(D) Neither misrepresentation nor tortious interference with contractual relations

156. What is the difference between tortious interference with contract and tortious interference with economic opportunity (or tortious interference with prospective economic advantage)?

ANSWER:

Nemo worked as a forklift operator for Rayon, Inc. One day he became injured while using the forklift. He received worker's compensation payments and also filed a products liability claim against Forko, the manufacturer of the forklift, alleging manufacturing defects. About a year later, while Nemo's claim was pending, Rayon Inc. hired an outside company, Timeshare Inc., to perform maintenance and cleanups at various worksites. Misunderstanding its work orders from Rayon Inc., Timeshare Inc. disassembled the forklift that had injured Nemo and had since been put into storage. This disassembly caused pieces of the forklift to be lost. With no forklift to examine, Nemo's products liability claim became unprovable and he had to withdraw it.

157. In an action against Timeshare, Inc., Nemo should

(A) prevail, because Timeshare assumed a duty of care, breached it, and caused financial loss to Nemo.

(B) prevail, because Timeshare exceeded the scope of its employment and caused financial loss to Nemo.

(C) not prevail, unless Nemo can prove aggravation of physical injuries.

(D) not prevail, unless Nemo can prove an undertaking.

158. Which of the following arguments provides the WEAKEST support for making tort liability available to remedy economic loss caused by negligence when plaintiff and defendant are not united by a contract?

(A) The extent of liability expands in nearly infinite chain reactions of economic harm.

(B) The defendant is by hypothesis negligent and its negligence has caused economic harm.

(C) The defendant will frequently be underdeterred from negligent behavior, absent such liability.

(D) The plaintiff will frequently lack adequate alternative sources of compensation for injury that it cannot prevent through reasonable care.

159. Which of the following illustrates a claim of strict liability for misrepresentation that could succeed?

(A) Genevieve showed Barton a surveyor's map of her land and told him that according to this map that she had commissioned, the land had unobstructed access to a lake. Barton inferred that the land had access to the lake and bought it from Genevieve. It turned out that the surveyor had surveyed the land inaccurately: the land did not have access to the lake. Barton suffered a financial loss. Barton brought an action against Genevieve.

(B) A state statute requires that all fruits and vegetables treated with the pesticide CREECH must disclose this condition on a label. Alfred, a grocer, bought vegetables from a reputable organic grower and inspected them for pesticide residue. The vegetables appeared to be free of pesticides. Alfred sold them unlabeled. It turned out that a carrier had switched some boxes and the vegetables were indeed treated with CREECH. A customer suffered a reaction to CREECH after eating the vegetables, and brought an action against Alfred.

(C) Dalma hired Enron Auditors to prepare financial statements about her business when she was offering it for sale. Enron Auditors prepared statements that significantly overstated the value of the business, causing injury to the buyer, an investor who lived out of state. When she hired Enron Auditors, Dalma knew that they had a reputation for producing inflated, "rosy scenario" financial statements. This reputation was not widely known beyond Dalma's community. The buyer brought an action against Dalma.

(D) Robin sincerely believed that the prize heifer she was selling had no diseases. A reasonable person experienced in dealing with heifers would have realized that the appearance of Robin's heifer indicated a congenital defect. Endora bought Robin's heifer, and like Robin took no notice of the telltale appearance of the heifer. The heifer turned out to have a disease related to the congenital defect and Endora suffered financial loss. Endora brought an action against Robin.

Q and E are parties to a contract. S induces Q to breach the contract with E, causing financial loss to E. E brings an action of tortious interference with contract against S. S contends that E must bring an action against Q for breach of contract, either before or during the suit against S, before any judgment can be entered against S.

160. Is S wrong?

ANSWER:

Lawyer Llewellyn represented client Carmen in her attempts to collect on a succession of ill-fated loans. He filed lawsuits against the debtors, with only partial success. One of Carmen's debtors, Dravath, agreed to pay a reduced amount in settlement of Carmen's claim. Llewellyn prepared a settlement agreement, to be signed by Carmen and Dravath. In this settlement agreement, which Llewellyn himself typed in haste, the amount that Dravath agreed to pay, which should have been $820,000, was recorded as $280,000. Llewellyn gave the document to Carmen to review; Carmen, also hurrying, did not notice the error, and signed it. (Dravath signed it too, although what he knew or noticed at the time is unknown.) Llewellyn had several occasions to catch the error before filing the agreement, but did not proofread the document at any time before filing it. Relying on the erroneous rendering of the settlement amount, the court in which the agreement was filed determined that Carmen could receive only $280,000 instead of $820,000 from Dravath. In an action for legal malpractice by Carmen against Llewellyn for the difference between the two sums, a judge would note Carmen's failure to spot the error before signing the agreement.

161. Which of the following statements best describes the proper judicial response to this failure of Carmen's?

(A) The error should have no effect on Carmen's claim for legal malpractice.

(B) The error may be considered contributory or comparative negligence.

(C) The error may be considered contributory or comparative negligence if Llewellyn can establish that Carmen would have otherwise been able to collect the full amount of the settlement.

(D) Because Carmen had the last clear chance to avoid harmful consequences, the error should defeat Carmen's claim against Llewellyn.

162. In a claim for tortious interference with contract, can a plaintiff recover for his emotional and reputational harm as well as his financial loss? What is the contrary argument?

ANSWER:

Thousands of residents of Wilkaukee became severely ill with diarrhea and other intestinal problems over a period of several days. A city investigation revealed that the drinking water had become contaminated with a bacterium. Almost everyone who became ill recovered fully within a few days, but for people with weak immune systems, the problem was much more serious. One such person was Arni, an AIDS patient whose immune system was extremely weak. Arni died from the bacterial infection brought on by the drinking water. Arni's estate has sued the city of Wilkaukee for negligence. Assume Wilkaukee is not immune.

163. Based only on the facts given, which of the following arguments could the city use?

(A) Because Arni was extra sensitive, the action should fail.

(B) The water contamination was not the cause in fact of Arni's death.

(C) Because AIDS almost certainly would have shortened Arni's life, he suffered no damage.

(D) Because AIDS almost certainly would have shortened Arni's life, his damages should be reduced.

164. Should plaintiffs get to keep punitive damages awards, or should these awards be allotted to some defined public purpose? If you favor the latter choice, what is the most appropriate public purpose? Discuss.

ANSWER:

165. A car driven negligently by Doe repeatedly collided with Preston's car. Preston sues for negligence. Which of the following statements is accurate?

(A) If Preston proves physical injury as a result of the collisions, he may recover emotional distress damages regardless of the rule followed in the jurisdiction concerning the tort of negligent infliction of emotional distress.

(B) If emotional distress was not a reasonably foreseeable consequence of causing these collisions, Preston cannot recover for the emotional distress.

(C) Because Preston's injuries did not result from observation of Doe's negligent injury of another person, Preston cannot recover for the emotional distress.

(D) If Preston had a preexisting condition that made him particularly susceptible to suffering emotional distress in an auto accident, Preston cannot recover for the emotional distress.

166. Which of the following types of damages should generally be discounted to present value?

(A) Damages recoverable under the collateral source rule

(B) Damages for past pain and suffering

(C) Lost future earnings damages

(D) Punitive damages

167. For most tort claims, a plaintiff has a duty to mitigate damages. To which of the following claims does this rule NOT apply?

(A) 'Wrongful formation' of a child, due to negligence in sterilization surgery

(B) A 'second injury' claim where a plaintiff has been injured due to the negligence of two defendants acting separately

(C) Tortious interference with contract

(D) Negligent failure to diagnose a life-threatening condition

168. Define and explain the collateral source rule.
ANSWER:

169. Which of the following social problems is LEAST relevant to the tort reform endeavor of reducing the amount of damages plaintiffs can seek in court?

(A) The refusal of insurance companies to write or renew malpractice insurance policies for physicians.

(B) The prosecution of marginal personal injury claims.

(C) The reluctance of manufacturing businesses to market useful products.

(D) The difficulty of identifying the optimal percentage of a judgment or settlement for the purpose of fixing a contingency fee.

Jessamyn purchased a Tootlin' TX model sport utility vehicle from a retail dealer. Within a year of the sale, the entire body of the Tootlin' TX was covered in rust. She brought an action against the manufacturer, TTX Inc. It emerged in discovery that TTX Inc. had used on 500 of its Tootlin' TXs an inferior grade of paint that it had bought very cheaply from a disreputable supplier. An internal document revealed that TTX Inc. had recommended to dealers that these inferior vehicles be sold "whenever possible" to women, minorities, and customers likely not to qualify for favorable financing, because "they're too intimidated to complain and they don't know the [state] 'lemon laws'." A jury awarded Jessamyn $30,000 in compensatory damages and $80,000 in punitive damages.

170. Is the punitive damages portion of the award proper under the Supreme Court standard expressed in BMW of North America, Inc. v. Gore, 116 S. Ct. 1589 (1996)?

(A) Yes, because a jury could reasonably find that TTX Inc. acted with actual malice.

(B) Yes, because TTX Inc.'s behavior is reprehensible, the ratio of punitive to compensatory damages is not too high, and potential sanctions for comparable misconduct are likely to be similar.

(C) No, because this standard pertains only to personal injury damages, not the property damage experienced here.

(D) No, because punitive damages claims are preempted by deceptive trade practices statutes like "lemon laws."

171. For cases involving permanent disabling injury, give arguments for and against allowing a plaintiff's lawyer to argue to jurors that they should fix the future pain and suffering award based on something like "Calculate the dollar value of the amount of pain [name of plaintiff] suffers each day, then multiply it by the number of days [the plaintiff] is expected to live."

ANSWER:

172. In which of the following cases would a court be most likely to award nominal damages, relieving the plaintiff from the burden of showing actual loss or injury?

(A) *Estevez v. New York Empire*. The plaintiff is the president of the United States and the defendant is a New York newspaper. Estevez objects to an Empire news story claiming that he had been treated for depression with electroshock therapy. The story is false: Estevez had been treated for depression with a combination of tranquilizers and muscle relaxants that are frequently used in conjunction with electroshock treatment. A psychiatrist reviewing files for the Empire story had inferred that Estevez must have been receiving electroshock therapy, and told the Empire reporter that Estevez had indeed received such treatment.

(B) *Susquehanna v. Lackawanna*. The parties' own adjacent lands. Lackawanna installed a tool shed at the edge of her property that protruded into Susquehanna's land. After receiving two threatening letters from Susquehanna, Lackawanna took down the tool shed.

(C) *Grossnickel v. Wilcox.* The parties both reside in separate, adjacent condominium units in the Waterhole, a fashionable high-rise. Wilcox enjoys a hobby of attempting to make perfume at home. The resulting odors sicken Grossnickel and have caused him to work less well in his Waterhole home office, causing lost income.

(D) *Dumm v. Bummer.* Dumm, the plaintiff, suffered severe emotional distress when she saw the defendant, Bummer, ride his motorcycle negligently over the foot of her husband. Dumm heard what she described as "the crunch of bone." She has suffered sleep disturbances, but no physical injury.

Ermintrude sues Needlenose and Ludwig for negligence. Ermintrude's case goes to the jury, and the jury determines that Ermintrude suffered $10,000 in damages but that all three parties failed to exercise reasonable care. The jury assesses Ludwig's fault at 50% of the total, Needlenose's fault at 15% of the total, and Ermintrude's fault at 35% of the total.

173. If the jurisdiction has adopted a pure form of comparative negligence, but has not abolished the common law rule concerning joint and several liability, which of the following statements is correct?

   (A) Ermintrude will receive a judgment for $6500 against both Ludwig and Needlenose, and may choose to recover all or part of that sum from either or both defendant.

   (B) Ermintrude will receive a judgment for $5000 against Ludwig and $1500 against Needlenose.

   (C) Ermintrude will receive a judgment of $10,000 against both Ludwig and Needlenose, and may choose to recover all or part of that sum from either or both defendants.

   (D) Ermintrude will receive a judgment of $5000 against Ludwig, but nothing against Needlenose because her negligence exceeded his.

174. Describe the most significant type of vicarious liability recognized by tort law.
ANSWER:

Bender picked up Fry on the way to the park, where they planned to play basketball. Excited about the game, Bender lost concentration on his driving and collided with a car driven by Hermes, who had stopped at a red light.

175. Hermes sues Bender and Fry. Concerning *Fry's* liability, which of the following statements is most accurate?

   (A) Unless Hermes can demonstrate that Fry acted negligently in some manner, Fry cannot be held liable.

   (B) Because Bender and Fry were involved in a joint venture, Fry can be held vicariously liable for Bender's negligence.

   (C) If Fry was aware that Bender was a bad driver, Fry can be held liable to Hermes.

   (D) Because the danger associated with careless driving outweighs any benefit to be obtained from the basketball game, Fry and Bender can both be held liable to Hermes, an innocent victim.

176. What is the difference between "contribution" and "indemnity"?
ANSWER:

Stingray was a passenger in a car driven by Hiram. Hiram negligently caused an accident, then fled the scene without helping Stingray. After half an hour, a passerby arrived and transported Stingray to the hospital. Unfortunately, Dr. Zoid, the emergency room doctor, negligently injured Stingray's back while attempting to move him onto a hospital bed.

177. If Stingray sues both Zoid and Hiram for the back injury, which of the following statements is most accurate?

(A) Only Hiram will be held liable.

(B) Only Zoid will be held liable.

(C) Both will be held liable.

(D) Neither will be held liable because it is impossible to apportion the injury between the two defendants.

In the 1990s, a jury convicted Charles Ng of eleven murders committed during 1984 and 1985. At the time of the murders, Ng was in his early 20s. At the sentencing phase, the defense presented evidence that Ng's father beat Ng severely when he was a boy. Suppose the estate of one of Ng's victims files a wrongful death action against Ng's father, alleging that his beatings contributed to Ng's later violence. The underlying tort is negligence. Assume research shows a relationship between child abuse and later violent behavior by the abused person.

178. Which of the following statements is correct?

(A) Because Ng was not a child when he murdered plaintiff's deceased, the father cannot be held liable.

(B) Because the father is not vicariously liable for the acts of his adult child, the father cannot be held liable.

(C) The father cannot be held liable because Ng's criminal behavior broke the chain of causation between the father's wrongdoing and the murder.

(D) The father can be held liable even though he was not directly involved in the murder.

179. How does respondeat superior resemble strict products liability?
ANSWER:

Darren owns First Step, a board and care facility for mental patients who have been confined in a state hospital but who have been deemed ready for a measure of independence. One night, Endora, a resident of First Step, climbed out through a second-story window and attacked Jade, a pedestrian who was walking past the facility. Jade suffered cuts and bruises.

180. If Jade sues Darren, which of the following statements is most accurate?

(A) Unless Darren was negligent in supervising the residents at night, Jade will not be able to recover.

(B) Because Darren is vicariously responsible for Endora's tortious conduct that is a foreseeable consequence of her residency at First Step, Darren will be liable.

(C) Because Endora's criminal conduct superseded any negligence on Darren's part, Jade will not be able to recover.

(D) Because Darren negligently permitted Endora to escape, Darren will be liable.

181. Which of the following assertions is LEAST relevant to the debate over whether to abolish joint and several liability?

(A) Joint and several liability is inconsistent with the modern adoption of comparative fault.

(B) Joint and several liability assigns liability out of proportion to a defendant's degree of relative culpability.

(C) Joint and several liability compels solvent defendants to supply what insolvent or immune defendants do not contribute to an award of damages.

(D) Joint and several liability is imposed whether or not the plaintiff's fault contributed to the injury.

The state of Cranberry has retained joint liability while accepting percentage-based apportionment. In an action for negligence brought in a Cranberry court, Tyler was awarded a judgment of $1,000,000 against four defendants: Billiard, Mugwump, Orestes, and Wallawalla. The jury apportioned responsibility among the four defendants as follows: Billiard 30%, Mugwump 20%, Orestes 40%, and Wallawalla 10%. Mugwump is insolvent and cannot pay any portion of the judgment.

182. How much should Tyler collect from each defendant?

    (A) $400,000 from Orestes, $300,000 from Billiard, $200,000 from Mugwump, and $100,000 from Wallawalla

    (B) $500,000 from Orestes, $375,000 from Billiard, and $125,000 from Wallawalla

    (C) $400,000 from Orestes, $300,000 from Billiard, and $100,000 from Wallawalla

    (D) $480,000 from Orestes, $360,000 from Billiard, and $120,000 from Wallawalla

183. In claims of respondeat superior, who decides the question of whether an employee's act falls within the scope of employment: judge or jury?

ANSWER:

184. Parents are not generally liable for the torts of their children. What are the exceptions to this rule?

ANSWER:

PRACTICE FINAL EXAM

As Doug was driving along Main Street, he became distracted by his ringing cell phone and crossed the centerline, colliding with a car driven by Pearl. Pearl was uninjured, but her car's steering mechanism was damaged. Pearl tried to drive the car to a safe spot at the side of the road, but lost control along the way and ran directly into a utility pole, injuring herself. Pearl sues Doug for negligence.

185. If Doug claims he is not responsible for Pearl's injury, which of the following statements is most likely correct?

(A) If a reasonable person in Pearl's position, taking into account the emergency, would have been able to maneuver the car safely to the side of the road, Pearl's conduct will be treated as a superseding cause that absolves Doug of responsibility for her injury.

(B) If a reasonable person in Pearl's position, *not* taking into account the emergency, would have been able to maneuver the car safely to the side of the road, Pearl's conduct will be treated as a superseding cause that absolves Doug of responsibility for her injury.

(C) Because Pearl was acting to avoid the consequences of Doug's negligence, her conduct will not affect Doug's liability for her injury.

(D) Because Pearl was acting to avoid the consequences of Doug's negligence, her conduct will not absolve Doug of responsibility for her injury, but Pearl's recovery may be reduced if the jury finds her to have been contributorily negligent under the circumstances.

Whatsamatta U negligently maintained the electrical system in its law building. One day, a fire broke out, destroying the building as well as an adjacent house owned by Winkle. The next day, a raging forest fire swept out of the hills behind the campus and took a path directly through the place where Winkle's house had stood. The forest fire was started by Rocky, a smoker who threw a lit cigarette out of his car window. Whatsamatta U is insolvent. Winkle has sued Rocky for negligence, seeking to recover the value of his burned house.

186. Which of the following statements is most accurate?

(A) Because the house was not destroyed by the fire Rocky started, Rocky will prevail.

(B) Because Winkle cannot prove that Rocky's fire would have destroyed the house, Rocky will prevail.

(C) Because Rocky is a negligent party, the law will not permit him to shield himself behind the fortuitous fact that his fire came after the one caused by Whatsamatta U. Therefore, Winkle will prevail.

(D) Because Whatsamatta U is insolvent and Winkle is an innocent party, Rocky will be held liable.

Manu owned a factory that used toxic chemicals. One day, an employee was moving a drum of chemicals using a forklift when, due to no negligence on Manu's part, the drum rolled off the forklift, crashed through a fence separating Manu's land from that of Pam, who owned a soybean farm, and split open, spilling chemicals on the land and killing some of Pam's crops. Manu immediately sent workers to Pam's land to clean up the spill, but the heavy equipment used by the workers destroyed some of Pam's crops that the chemical would not have damaged. Pam sues Manu for trespass to recover for the damage caused to her crops by the heavy equipment.

187. Which of the following statements is most likely correct?

(A) Because Manu's employees voluntarily went onto Pam's land, Manu is liable for trespass.

(B) Because Manu's conduct created the situation that made its employees' entry necessary, Manu cannot argue that it was privileged to enter Pam's land by the doctrine of necessity.

(C) Because it was necessary to enter Pam's land to minimize property damage, Manu was privileged to enter and so did not commit a trespass. Even so, it will be required to pay for the harm.

(D) Because it was necessary to enter Pam's land to minimize property damage, Manu was privileged to enter and so did not commit a trespass. Therefore, Manu will not be required to pay for the harm.

Myringotomy is one of the most common types of surgery in the United States. Usually performed on young children who suffer from chronic ear infections that can cause permanent ear damage, the surgery involves placing tiny tubes in the eardrums to allow fluid to escape, preventing the onset of ear infections. Because the ear is delicate, surgeons customarily use a light general anesthetic on children who might move around too much if they are awake during the procedure. Aside from risks normally associated with general anesthesia, a rare risk of the surgery is that the tubes will permanently damage the eardrums.

Carla, age 4, had already had many serious ear infections and did not respond well to antibiotics. Her pediatrician recommended that she see Gary, an ear specialist, to determine whether she should undergo a myringotomy. After examining Carla and consulting with her parents, Gary recommended the surgery. He told Carla's parents exactly what the surgery entailed, as well as its risks and benefits and the risks and benefits of the other alternatives. In keeping with medical custom, however, he did not tell Carla herself that the surgery involved puncturing her eardrums to insert tiny tubes. The parents approved the surgery.

Just before the surgery was to begin, Carla became very frightened when she overheard some nurses discussing the nature of the surgery. Before Carla could say she didn't want to go through with it, a mask was placed over her face and she was off to dreamland. During the surgery Gary used a larger tube than is customarily used for children of Carla's size, and when he inserted it in her right ear, the large hole it made permanently impaired Carla's hearing in that ear.

188. If Carla wishes to sue Gary, which of the following theories has the greatest chance of success?

(A) Battery, for performing surgery against her wishes.

(B) Negligence, for using a tube larger than that customarily used in the profession.

(C) Assault, for causing Carla's apprehension of suffering imminent harmful or offensive contact.

(D) Carla does not have any chance of recovery based on any tort theory.

Wynona Law School was building a new parking garage. The land was cleared and work began on shoring the perimeter with concrete columns sunk thirty feet into the ground. Much heavy equipment was needed, including a number of special concrete mixers, one of which was very valuable. Each night, workers would suspend that mixer about fifteen feet in the air on a cable attached to a construction crane. Late one night, as a prank, law students Adam and Eve painted the words "FRAT MIXER" on a large piece of cardboard, climbed over the six-foot fence separating the construction site from the rest of the property, and hoisted the sign onto the mixer. As they were leaving, a sudden and powerful wind gust caused the mixer to swing wildly on the cable from which it was suspended. Adam was injured when a metal part broke off the mixer and struck him in the head. Adam has sued Wynona Law School for negligence to recover for his injury. Assume the state in which the action is filed adheres to traditional rules regarding the liability of land owners and occupiers.

189. Which of the following states the most likely outcome of Adam's action?

(A) Wynona will be liable for negligence because it is unreasonable to leave equipment where it could swing in a wind and injure someone on or off the property.

(B) Wynona will not be liable for negligence because its negligent act was not the cause in fact of Adam's injury.

(C) Wynona will not be liable for negligence because it had no duty to protect Adam from the harm that occurred.

(D) It is not possible to predict the outcome of this case without additional information.

190. Same facts as in Question 189. Assume for purposes of this question that the state in which the action is filed has abolished the common law rules governing the liability of landowners and occupiers. Which of the following states the most likely outcome of Adam's action?

(A) Wynona will be liable for negligence because it is unreasonable to leave equipment where it could swing in a wind and injure someone on or off the property.

(B) Wynona will not be liable for negligence because its negligent act was not the cause in fact of Adam's injury.

(C) Wynona will not be liable for negligence because it had no duty to protect Adam from the harm that occurred.

(D) It is not possible to predict the outcome of this case without additional information.

District Attorney Drucilla was sick and tired of divorced parents falling behind on court-ordered child support payments. To crack down on these "deadbeat parents," Drucilla rented a large billboard in a prominent location. Each month, the billboard featured a photo of the "Deadbeat Parent of the Month" and a statement of how much the person owed for child support. For April, Drucilla chose Walrus, a businessperson who owed more than $20,000 in child support. Unfortunately, the Walrus whose photograph was used on the billboard was not the Walrus who owed the money. The photo, instead, depicted a prominent psychiatrist. When psychiatrist Walrus learned of the poster, he suffered serious emotional distress, eventually leading to the breakup of his marriage. He became a shut-in, refusing to leave his luxury condo. He has sued Drucilla in her official capacity as D.A. Assume Drucilla failed to exercise reasonable care to ensure that the correct photograph was selected, and that she is not immune from suit.

191. Which cause of action best suits the facts?
ANSWER:

A 1997 Canadian study published in the *New England Journal of Medicine* concluded that a driver is four times more likely to get into an accident while talking on a cell phone or while legally drunk than if she is doing neither. Clifford's luxury car came equipped with a cell phone. One morning, while driving along a busy highway during rush hour and using his cell phone, he was involved in a collision with Norm, whose car was using the lane to Clifford's left. Norm was driving carefully. Both drivers were injured. Norm has sued Clifford for negligence.

192. If Norm establishes that Clifford was not acting reasonably when he used the cell phone under these circumstances, which of the following statements is most likely correct?

    (A) Clifford will be liable for Norm's damages if Norm demonstrates that the use of the cell phone was a cause in fact and proximate cause of the collision.

    (B) Clifford will prevail because the risks associated with using cell phones on busy roads is well known.

    (C) The burden of persuasion on the issue of causation will shift to Clifford, who was negligent and possessed the greatest amount of information on the causation issue.

    (D) Clifford will not be liable for Norm's damages because he was using an appliance that was legally installed in his car.

Demetria witnessed a murder, and told Detective Richards that Frank was the killer. Richards told Demetria about a witness protection program and said that, if a witness is threatened, she will be relocated. Frank was arrested, charged with murder, and jailed. Soon, an anonymous caller told Demetria that if she testified, her home would be blown up. Demetria told Richards about the call, and Richards advised Demetria to contact him if the threats continued. Though Richards believed the threat was coming from the jailed Frank or Frank's family or friends, and though Richards believed Frank to be dangerous, he did not tell Demetria that Frank was a suspect in other murders or that he had threatened witnesses in those other cases. Just before she was to testify at Frank's trial, associates of Frank murdered Demetria while she was waiting for a bus. Though Frank was still in jail, he ordered the killing.

193. Demetria's estate has sued the city for negligence based on the actions of Detective Richards. The city might claim it had no duty to warn Demetria or act to prevent her murder. Dispute this contention about no duty.

ANSWER:

194. Same facts as in Question 193. If the city contends that it owed Demetria a duty of care, but claims it satisfied its duty by confining Frank, which of the following statements is most accurate?

    (A) Because Frank was jailed at the relevant times, the city satisfied its duty as a matter of law.

    (B) Because Demetria was killed despite the fact that Frank was jailed at the relevant times, the city breached its duty as a matter of law.

    (C) The court should allow the jury to determine whether the city breached its duty.

    (D) The court will shift to the city the burden of demonstrating that it did not breach its duty.

195. Same facts as in Question 193. The city claims that Demetria assumed the risk by riding public transportation after receiving a death threat and shortly before she was scheduled to testify against a person charged with murder. Which of the following statements is most accurate?

    (A) It would be reasonable for a jury to decide that Demetria assumed the risk in the primary sense, eliminating any duty the city owed to her.

    (B) It would be reasonable for a jury to decide that Demetria assumed the risk in the secondary sense, thereby reducing any possible recovery.

    (C) Because Demetria's decision to ride public transportation was unreasonable and was a causal factor in her death, any discussion of assumption of risk is unnecessary.

    (D) The court should rule as a matter of law that Demetria did not assume the risk.

The rock concert was sold out, but Diva went to the stadium hoping to buy a ticket from a scalper just before the show. Scalpers' prices were higher than Diva could afford, and Diva began to walk back to her car, dejected. Suddenly, Diva had an idea. She ran toward Pluto, who was holding his ticket, waiting to enter the arena, and let out a blood-curdling scream. As Pluto turned to check out the noise, he saw Diva rushing toward him. Diva reached him within a couple of seconds, grabbed his ticket and ran toward the entrance. Pluto started after her, but could not catch up.

196. If Pluto sues Diva for assault, which of the following statements is most accurate?

    (A) Because Diva touched an object closely connected with Pluto's person (the ticket), Pluto's proper cause of action would be for battery. Therefore, Pluto's assault action will not succeed.

    (B) Because Pluto was not frightened by Diva, Pluto's assault action will not succeed.

    (C) By holding his ticket in a manner that would allow someone to grab it, Pluto assumed the risk. Therefore, his assault action will not succeed.

    (D) Pluto's assault action will probably succeed.

197. Same facts as in Question 196. Suppose Pluto had reacted very quickly to Diva's rapid approach, and had struck her with his fist just as she reached him, knocking her down and bruising her. If Diva sues Pluto for battery, and the case is tried to a jury, which of the following statements is most accurate?

(A) If the judge finds that Pluto reasonably believed Diva was going to batter him, and that Pluto did not use excessive force in repelling Diva, then she should enter judgment for Pluto.

(B) If the jury finds that Pluto reasonably believed Diva was going to batter him, and that Pluto did not use excessive force in repelling Diva, then it should render a verdict for Pluto.

(C) If the judge finds that Diva did not intend to touch Pluto, she should hold Pluto liable.

(D) If the jury finds that Diva did not intend to touch Pluto, it should hold Pluto liable.

Gamblers' Express (GE) runs package tours for senior citizens from River City to Lost Wages, a gambling resort. GE is *not* a public carrier. Eliot, age 79, signed up for an excursion and boarded the bus one Tuesday morning. A few minutes before the bus was scheduled for a rest stop, George, a 75-year-old passenger sitting just behind Eliot, got up to remove an item from the overhead bin. While George was still standing, Marny, the driver, pulled the bus to the side of the road so she could open an overhead air vent. (The air conditioner broke an hour out of River City.) Unfortunately, Marny did not tell the passengers at the beginning of the trip to stay seated at all times, and she failed to check her mirror to see if anybody was standing in the aisle before she pulled over. As the bus came to a stop, George lost his balance and fell into Eliot, injuring Eliot's shoulder.

198. If Eliot wishes to sue George, which of the following theories is most viable on the law and supported by the facts?

(A) Battery, based on the theory that George should have recognized he was substantially certain to lose his balance and fall into another passenger.

(B) Battery, based on the theory that George knew his age made him more prone to falling than a younger person.

(C) Negligence, based on the theory that a reasonable person in George's position, taking account of his age and health, would not have stood up while the bus was moving.

(D) Negligence, based on the theory that a reasonable person of average age and health would not have stood up while the bus was moving.

Augustine owned August Summer Bakery Inc., a small business. Her cousin Kermit, who had worked in the bakery as a child, was interested in buying it from Augustine when she retired. Kermit and Augustine had chatted off and on for ten years about how the bakery would transfer eventually from Augustine to Kermit, although they never reduced their conversations to writing. The two were never close, despite their familial relationship. While Augustine operated the bakery, her neighbor John decided he wanted to buy it. He worried that Augustine would favor Kermit over him as a buyer. To induce Augustine to sell the bakery to him instead, John told Augustine a true story she did not know: Kermit had pleaded guilty to charges related to child abuse fifteen years earlier. Augustine was horrified and decided to sell the bakery to John instead of Kermit.

199. These facts might give rise to a claim by Kermit against John for

    (A) tortious interference with prospective economic opportunity.

    (B) tortious interference with contract.

    (C) defamation.

    (D) invasion of privacy.

Huckleberry was a passenger on a tour bus owned and operated by Bus Co. (not a common carrier). At one point, the driver pulled over to the side of the road so she could fix something on her uniform, which had become uncomfortable. While the bus was stopped, it was struck from the rear by another vehicle. Huckleberry was injured when the collision caused him to hit his head on a metal bar. Huckleberry sues Bus Co. for negligence, alleging that the driver had a duty not to stop the bus except at designated rest stops and that she breached her duty by stopping when she did. Bus Co. regulations provide that drivers must stop only at designated rest stops.

200. Which of the following statements is accurate?

    (A) Because the driver's conduct violated company regulations, her actions were a superseding cause of Huckleberry's harm, defeating Huckleberry's claim.

    (B) If the jurisdiction follows a "scope of risk" theory, the driver's conduct, if negligent, would be viewed as a superseding cause, defeating Huckleberry's claim.

    (C) Because the driver's conduct constituted an intentional tort, Bus Co. may not be held vicariously liable.

    (D) If the driver's conduct was unreasonable, Huckleberry can recover against Bus Co.

In the last few seconds of a professional hockey game, Gilles, a player whose team trailed by one point hit a hard shot toward the goal from a great distance. A long shot in every sense of the word, this was a desperate effort to tie the game. The puck missed the goal and flew into the stands, striking Fred, whose seat was several rows up from the ice. Fred sues Gilles.

201. Which of the following statements is most accurate?

    (A) Because Gilles knew with substantial certainty that the puck would strike somebody if it did not go into the goal, he will be liable for battery.

(B) Because Gilles should have known with substantial certainty that the puck would strike somebody if it did not go into the goal, he will be liable for battery.

(C) Because Gilles negligently hit the puck, he will be liable for negligence.

(D) Gilles will prevail.

Vlad knew nothing about the rules of hockey, had never attended a game, and had no idea that pucks can fly off the ice and into the stands. Vlad went with some friends to a professional game at a stadium owned and operated by HockeyCo. Vlad spent his time talking to his friends and paid little attention to the game. At one point, a puck flew off the ice and struck Vlad, injuring him. Vlad sues HockeyCo for negligence, alleging that HockeyCo should have constructed a higher barrier that would protect him from flying pucks. The barrier used by HockeyCo was the same height as barriers used in all other hockey stadiums at which professional teams play.

202. Which of the following statements is most accurate?

(A) Vlad will not recover because HockeyCo did not owe him a duty to protect him from this kind of injury.

(B) Vlad's recovery should be reduced because, even though HockeyCo was negligent, he confronted a danger of which most people are aware.

(C) Vlad's recovery should be reduced because he was comparatively negligent for choosing a seat that was not protected by the barrier.

(D) Vlad will recover fully for his injuries.

203. Which of the following scenarios illustrates negligent (as compared with intentional) defamation?

(A) Libby, desiring to injure the reputation of her sorority sister Sondra, wrote graffiti on a campus restroom wall alleging that Sondra was sexually promiscuous.

(B) Morticia, editor of a small neighborhood weekly newspaper, ran a story without editing it, because she was too busy that day with personal matters to do her job. The story reported an accusation of sexual assault. Contrary to the newspaper's policy, and much to the dismay of Morticia, the story included the name of the accuser.

(C) Real estate broker Sheraton sends a monthly letter to clients and potential clients describing his recent successes. In his last letter, Sheraton forgot to mention having sold Gabriel's house. Gabriel infers that Sheraton wishes to dissociate himself from the sale, thereby impugning Gabriel and his house.

(D) Because of an intern's shakiness with numbers and tendency to transpose by mistake, a newspaper published a story saying that Wimpy's restaurant scored 49 on a health inspection. The restaurant actually scored 94. A score below 70 is considered failing.

Steve and Rose were playing tag in the park. Steve spotted Rose, and moved slowly toward her to tag her. Rose moved backward to avoid Steve. Steve knew Rose was nearing the edge of the sidewalk and a rather high curb, and he sensed that Rose was not aware of these facts. Nevertheless, he continued to advance. Rose stumbled over the curb and fell into the street, suffering several cuts on her arms and head. Rose sues Steve for assault to recover for the fear she suffered as Steve slowly advanced toward her, just before she fell into the street.

204. Which of the following statements is most accurate?

(A) Because Steve acted with intent to cause apprehension of imminent contact, and because Rose suffered such apprehension, Steve is liable.

(B) If Rose knew she could avoid Steve's touch by simply running around him, Steve will not be liable.

(C) Because Steve was privileged to commit the touch that his actions threatened, he did not possess unlawful intent and will not be liable.

(D) Without more facts, it is not possible to determine whether Steve is likely to be liable to Rose for assault.

Norm was driving near a park. Though the speed limit was 25 mph, he was going 45 mph. Just after he rounded a corner, a child named Ronnie, who had been playing in the park, fell into the street. Norm did not see Ronnie in time to stop, and struck her. Had Norm been traveling 25 mph or less, he would have been able to stop in time. Ronnie sues Norm for battery.

205. Which of the following statements is most accurate?

(A) Because Norm was intentionally driving the car at the time and place and in the manner he was driving, and because he struck Ronnie, Norm will be liable.

(B) Because Norm should have known the grave risk of striking a child if he drove at such a high speed near a park, Norm will be liable.

(C) Because Norm intentionally violated a statute designed to protect a class of persons that included Ronnie, Norm will be liable.

(D) Because Norm did not possess unlawful intent, Norm will not be liable.

Fortune Studios, a long-time producer of low budget films, decided to make a futuristic action-adventure. Large portions of the Fortune lot, located in a heavily populated part of River City, were covered with sets for the $120 million movie. The largest set was the "rocket way," a highway for rocket-powered cars. For authenticity, Fortune used actual rocket engines to power the cars. The climactic chase scene was to take place on the rocket way, and weeks were spent preparing the cars and planning the scene for verisimilitude and maximum safety. While one rocket car was being readied for a trial run, its engine suddenly ignited, and the car accelerated down the rocket way with no one at the controls. When the rocket way turned left at the end of the set, the car continued straight and crashed through the retaining wall and onto a nearby city street, where it struck Dan's car as he drove by. The rocket car was destroyed, as was Dan's beloved sports car. Somehow, Dan was not injured.

Dan has sued Fortune for negligence. At trial, Dan calls an expert who testifies that a reasonable film company would have built a stronger retaining wall along the rocket way. Fortune's expert testifies that the walls used were strong enough to withstand expected mishaps. Assume that, had the stronger wall been built, the rocket car would not have crashed through it and onto the city street.

206. Based on the law and on the facts given, which of the following jury instructions would be most justified?

(A) "Members of the jury, you must decide whether Fortune's failure to construct a stronger retaining wall was unreasonable under the circumstances."

(B) "Members of the jury, the court has determined that Fortune had a duty to construct a stronger retaining wall around the edges of the rocket way, and that it violated this duty. You must simply assess Dan's damages."

(C) "Members of the jury, Fortune had a duty to act in good faith and to the best of its ability in designing and constructing the retaining walls around the rocket way. You must determine whether Fortune exercised such care and, if so, to assess Dan's damages."

(D) "Members of the jury, you must decide whether Fortune had a duty to exercise reasonable care toward Dan in this situation. If you decide it did have such duty, you must determine whether it breached the duty and, if so, the amount of damages Dan is entitled to recover."

207. Same facts as in Question 206. Assume Fortune asks the court to instruct the jury that because this was the first special effects extravaganza it had made, Fortune's efforts should not be compared with those of experienced producers of such films. Which of the following statements is most likely correct?

(A) The instruction should not be given because the judge is not allowed to influence the jury with her view of the reasonableness of a party's actions.

(B) The instruction should be given because Fortune's lack of experience in making this type of film proves, as a matter of law, that Fortune was negligent for attempting to produce this kind of film.

(C) The instruction should not be given because Fortune had a duty to exercise the care and skill of a reasonable, experienced producer of special effects extravaganzas.

(D) The instruction should be given because it would not be fair to impose on Fortune a duty it would not have been possible for it to satisfy.

MotorCo was developing a new type of automobile engine at its plant in River City. Although the fuel source being tested was more explosive than gasoline, the engine, if successful, could help end the nation's dependence on oil as a fuel source. One day, a test car that was supposed to remain stationary while the engine ran suddenly shifted into gear, and the driverless car lurched forward, broke through a barrier separating the plant from the public highway, and struck a car driven by Potter that was traveling along the highway. Potter sues MotorCo on a theory of strict liability. Assume the case was being decided by Justice Blackburn, who wrote one of the opinions in Rylands v. Fletcher, L.R. 1 Ex. 265 (1866), *aff'd* LR 3 H.L. 330 (1868).

208. Which of the following statements best approximates what Justice Blackburn would say?

(A) Traffic on the highways cannot be conducted without exposing those upon them to the inevitable risk of accident. In the absence of negligence, therefore, MotorCo cannot be held responsible to Potter.

(B) Because MotorCo carried on its business in a densely populated part of River City, it was engaging in what might be termed a non-natural, or inappropriate use of its land. Therefore, MotorCo is prima facie answerable for all the natural consequences of its activity.

(C) Trespass is the direct and immediate application of force to the person or property of the plaintiff. Because the occurrence which damaged Potter's vehicle did not occur as the direct result of any action on the part of MotorCo, Potter can recover, if at all, only upon a showing of negligence.

(D) Because Potter did not take upon himself any risk of harm from these dangerous activities, if MotorCo's experimental cars are likely to do harm if they escape its land, Potter should recover even in the absence of negligence on MotorCo's part.

209. Same facts as in Question 208. Assume Potter's strict liability action against MotorCo is brought on an "abnormally dangerous activity" theory under *Restatement (Second) of Torts* §§ 519-520 (1965). Which of the following statements is most likely correct?

(A) Because MotorCo's activity caused harm to a person outside the property, MotorCo is strictly liable.

(B) If the social benefit that might be gained from MotorCo's efforts outweigh the risk created by the activity, MotorCo cannot be held strictly liable.

(C) Because the feature of the experimental car that made it dangerous was the explosiveness of the type of fuel being used, MotorCo cannot be held strictly liable.

(D) If MotorCo could have prevented the car from slipping into gear by the exercise of reasonable care, it is more likely that MotorCo will be held strictly liable.

Philip was driving east on Privet Drive one morning when he was struck by a car driven by Snape, who had crossed the centerline to avoid striking a black cat. Snape did not have a driver's license. Philip sues Snape for negligence, and claims that Snape should be held negligent per se because he drove without a license.

210. Discuss whether the doctrine of negligence per se applies to this situation.
ANSWER:

Sharon was mentally ill and had been institutionalized in a series of facilities over the years. Often, she would walk away from the facilities, become disoriented, and would have to be located and returned. If the facility was an unlocked one, she would simply leave; if it was a locked one, she would walk away when left unattended in an insecure place. At one point, the public guardian decided that Sharon needed to be in a locked facility, but the one chosen refused to accept her. Thus, she was placed in Serene Chateau, an unlocked facility operated by Jackson. Neither the public guardian nor Farr, Sharon's social worker, told Jackson that Sharon had a habit of leaving facilities or that she would become disoriented when she did so. A day after entering Serene Chateau, Sharon stole a car and left. She was arrested and returned. A few days later, at a meeting attended by Sharon, her parents, Jackson, Farr, and the public guardian, Sharon was told she had to stop walking out if she wanted to be allowed to stay at Serene Chateau. Sharon was told to ask permission if she wanted to leave. She agreed to the conditions. A few days later, Sharon was granted permission to leave Serene Chateau to go shopping, and was told to be back by 5:30 for dinner. She failed to return. Two days later, she appeared on the driveway of a home that adjoined the busy coast highway. The resident noticed that Sharon seemed "kind of wobbly," but refused to help her when she sought food. A few minutes later, Sharon walked onto the highway, where she was struck and gravely injured by an automobile.

Sharon has sued Farr (the social worker) and the state (Farr's employer), alleging that they were negligent for failing adequately to advise Serene Chateau of Sharon's tendency to walk away and become disoriented when she would do so. Assume defendants are not immune. (In the actual case, Brookhauser v. State, 13 Cal. Rptr. 2d 658 (Cal. Ct. App. 1992), the court held that the defendants were immune.)

211. Which of the following arguments on behalf of defendants is viable?

(A) Defendants did not have a duty to inform Serene Chateau of Sharon's tendencies.

(B) Even if they had a duty to warn Serene Chateau of Sharon's tendencies, defendants did not breach their duty.

(C) Defendants' conduct was not a "but-for" cause in fact of Sharon's harm.

(D) Sharon's own fault should reduce her recovery.

212. Same facts as in Question 211. Assume the defendants argue that, even if they should have provided the information to Serene Chateau, and even if their negligence was a cause in fact of the harm, they should not be held liable. If the jurisdiction in which the action is being tried has adopted a "directness" theory of proximate cause such as that espoused by Justice Andrews in Palsgraf v. Long Island R.R. Co., 248 N.Y. 339, 162 N.E. 99 (1928), which of the following statements best represents what the court is most likely to say?

(A) Because a reasonable person in the defendants' position would foresee harm resulting from the failure to provide the information, the defendants were negligent. They are then liable for the full extent of the harm because the harm that occurred was precisely what one might expect to occur.

(B) Because a reasonable person in the defendants' position would foresee harm resulting from the failure to provide the information, the defendants were negligent. They are then liable for the full extent of the harm if the consequences that actually occurred followed directly from the negligence.

(C) Because a reasonable person in the defendants' position would foresee harm resulting from the failure to provide the information, the defendants were negligent. However, because the harm came about as an immediate consequence of Sharon's own carelessness, the harm was indirect and the defendants cannot be held liable.

(D) Because the zone of risk created by the defendants' carelessness included personal injury to Sharon, and because the manner in which Sharon was injured was precisely what one might reasonably foresee, the defendants are responsible for the full extent of the harm.

Same facts as in Question 211. Suppose the defendants wish to argue that, even if they should have provided the information to Serene Chateau, and even if their negligence was a cause in fact of the harm, they should not be held liable.

213. If the jurisdiction in which the action is being tried has adopted a "scope of risk" approach to proximate cause, which of the following statements best represents what the court is most likely to say?

(A) The test of liability for injury by highway accident is the foreseeability of injury by highway accident. Unless a reasonable person in the defendants' position could have foreseen injury of this kind to Sharon, she cannot recover.

(B) The test of liability for injury by highway accident is the foreseeability of injury by highway accident. Because no reasonable person in the defendants' position could have foreseen the chain of events that led to Sharon's injury, Sharon cannot recover.

(C) It would not be consonant with current ideas of justice or morality to hold a party responsible unless the harm occurred as a direct and natural consequence of its carelessness. Because the accident occurred through the intervention of both the driver of the car and of Sharon herself, the chain of causation was broken and Sharon cannot recover.

(D) It is not the hindsight of a fool but the foresight of a reasonable person that guides the determination of this question. Unless a reasonable person in the defendants' position could imagine that Sharon would suffer injury of this extent by virtue of the failure to provide the information to Serene Chateau, the defendants cannot be held responsible.

The state of Rhubarb has retained the common law categories of trespasser, licensee, and invitee. Muskrat, a wealthy resident of Rhubarb, decided to excavate a large stretch of his property in the back of his house in preparation for adding a new outbuilding on the land. He did not illuminate the excavated site of his land or post a warning sign. Muskrat's land is not fenced and, although he has not noticed any trespassers on his property, he has done nothing to keep them away. One night, teenage trespasser Tommy took a shortcut through Muskrat's land to hurry home after breaking curfew. Tommy fell into the excavation and was injured.

214. An action by Tommy against Muskrat should

(A) fail, because Tommy assumed the risk.

(B) fail, because Tommy was not a known trespasser.

(C) succeed, because it was negligent for Muskrat not to illuminate his property or warn visitors.

(D) succeed, because Tommy's trespassing was foreseeable.

Lois was on a walk when she noticed a very young child lying facedown and completely still in the yard in front of Peter's house. Believing the child was injured, Lois climbed the fence separating the sidewalk from the yard and approached him. When she touched his shoulder and asked if he was okay, the child turned over and said he was fine. Peter, the child's father, observed this activity from his front window and became extremely frightened because he believed Lois was accosting the child. Subsequently, he sued Lois for trespass.

215. Which of the following statements is most likely correct?

(A) The action will fail because Lois's entry onto Peter's property was not voluntary.

(B) The action will fail because Lois's trespass did not damage Peter's property.

(C) The action will fail because, under the circumstances, Lois's entry was not a trespass.

(D) The action will succeed.

216. Which subcategory of invasion of privacy has the greatest overlap with defamation? Explain.
ANSWER:

Dr. McAllister, a sinus specialist, recommended surgery to correct Kevin's deviated septum (the cartilage separating the nose into two segments), and to clear blocked passages. McAllister told Kevin the surgery would improve his breathing and help prevent lingering infections. Kevin asked McAllister what was involved in the surgery, and McAllister explained that the surgery was a very common, "endoscopic" procedure performed under general anesthesia, and that "few patients suffer any significant problems." Kevin asked what problems had arisen. McAllister said there were very rare cases in which surgeons punctured the patient's eye socket or caused brain damage by puncturing the brain cavity. He said he had performed the procedure hundreds of times without such mishaps. Kevin decided to go forward with the procedure.

McAllister did not disclose several possible side effects. Unfortunately, Kevin had some of them, including temporarily blocked sinuses, "adhesions" (tissue stuck together), numbness in his teeth, and severe pain. For a month, Kevin was in pain and couldn't concentrate at work. McAllister did what he could to relieve the side effects, but they did not disappear entirely for several months. Eventually, Kevin recovered completely, and he can breathe better than ever.

217. If Kevin wishes to proceed against Dr. McAllister on a theory of battery, which of the following statements is most likely accurate?

(A) Kevin can only prevail if he proves that his consent was ineffective because McAllister did not provide information that would have led Kevin not to consent to the surgery.

(B) Kevin can only prevail if he proves that his consent was ineffective because McAllister did not provide information that would have led a reasonable person not to consent to the surgery.

(C) Kevin cannot prevail because the surgery was effective to cure his sinus problems.

(D) Kevin cannot prevail because issues relating to a patient's consent to medical care can only be addressed by negligence principles.

218. Same facts as in Question 217. If Kevin sues McAllister for negligence, which of the following arguments would give McAllister's his best chance of defeating the claim?

(A) Kevin cannot recover because the undisclosed information did not relate to the surgery itself, only to the side effects.

(B) Kevin cannot recover because, even though he suffered pain from various side effects of the surgery, the pain was more than offset by the beneficial effects of the procedures.

(C) Kevin cannot recover if a reasonable patient in his position would not have considered the undisclosed information material to a decision whether to have the surgery.

(D) Kevin cannot recover if physicians in McAllister's position customarily do not disclose the information about the side effects that affected Kevin.

219. Same facts as in Question 217. If Kevin sues McAllister for negligence, and McAllister wishes to testify that he decided not to reveal the information in question to Kevin because he feared Kevin might make the irrational decision not to have the surgery, which of the following statements is most likely correct?

(A) The court should not allow McAllister to present this testimony because his views are irrelevant to the determination of negligence.

(B) The court should not allow McAllister to present this testimony because the patient's right to self-determination overrides the physician's views of the patient's "best interests."

(C) McAllister should be permitted to present this testimony if he thinks Kevin will forgo the procedure if informed of the side effects.

(D) McAllister should be permitted to present this testimony if it represents a sound medical judgment that providing the information would present a threat to Kevin's well being.

220. Same facts as in Question 217. Assume Kevin proceeds on a negligence theory. McAllister claims that, even if he had a duty to disclose the side effects and breached it by failing to disclose them, Kevin cannot prove the breach was a cause in fact of the harm. Which of the following statements is most accurate?

(A) Kevin can prove causation if he persuades the jury that he would not have undergone the surgery if McAllister had disclosed the side effects.

(B) Kevin can prove causation only if he persuades the jury that neither he nor a reasonable person would have undergone the surgery if McAllister had disclosed the side effects.

(C) Kevin can prove causation only if a reasonable person in McAllister's position would have foreseen harm resulting from failure to disclose the side effects.

(D) Kevin has shown causation once he demonstrates that McAllister breached his duty to disclose the side effects.

A sudden downpour soaked a ground already saturated from days of steady rain, threatening Wingnut City with serious flooding as the river began to rise. At the same time, the dam protecting the town began to crack from the pressure of water backed up in the lake behind it. Finally, the river overflowed its banks, and water began spreading through the town. At almost the same time, the dam burst, sending a torrent of water toward the town. A few blocks from Abel's art gallery, water from the river mixed with the water from the burst dam, and the flood bore down on the gallery, destroying all of Abel's valuable art. Later an investigation showed that the dam burst because of improper maintenance. Had the dam been maintained properly, it would have held the water back. Abel sues Wingnut City, which was responsible for maintaining the dam, for negligence. Assume either force standing alone (water from the river or the dam) would have been sufficient to destroy Abel's art collection. Assume also that Wingnut City is not immune.

221. Which of the following statements is most accurate?

(A) Because Abel's art gallery would have been flooded even without the city's negligence in maintaining the dam, Wingnut City's failure to maintain the dam was not a cause in fact of Abel's damage and is not liable.

(B) Wingnut City's failure to maintain the dam will be considered a cause in fact of the damage only if Abel can show that the volume of water from the dam that reached his gallery was greater than the volume of water from the river that reached his gallery.

(C) Wingnut City is liable only for the portion of the harm that corresponds to the percentage of water flooding Abel's gallery that came from the dam.

(D) Wingnut City's failure to maintain the dam was a cause in fact of the harm and the City is liable for all of the harm Abel suffered.

Same facts as in Question 221, except assume that water from the dam reached Abel's gallery and destroyed Abel's artwork about an hour before the river water inundated the property. If the dam had held, Abel would have had time to remove some of his goods from the gallery before the river water inundated it.

222. Discuss the possible damages for which Wingnut City might be liable.
ANSWER:

ChemCo negligently allowed a tank of chemicals to leak. Platt lived two miles from the ChemCo plant. Six months later, Platt became ill with a rare form of cancer.

223. If Platt wishes to recover from ChemCo, and ChemCo claims it was not the cause in fact of Platt's harm, what must Platt prove in order to overcome this contention?
ANSWER:

Steve and Rose were playing tag in the park. Steve spotted Rose, and moved slowly toward her to tag her. Rose moved backward to avoid Steve. Steve knew Rose was nearing the edge of the sidewalk and a rather high curb, and he sensed that Rose was not aware of these facts. Nevertheless, he continued to advance. Rose stumbled over the curb and fell into the street, suffering several cuts on her arms and head. Rose sues Steve for battery to recover for cuts on her arms and head as a result of her fall into the street.

224. Which of the following statements is most accurate?

(A) Because Steve did not intend to make Rose fall, Steve will not be liable.

(B) Because Steve was privileged to touch Rose under the circumstances, Steve will not be liable.

(C) If Steve knew it was substantially certain that Rose would trip over the edge of the sidewalk, Steve will be liable.

(D) If Steve should have known that it was substantially certain that Rose would trip over the edge of the sidewalk and suffer some physical injury, Steve will be liable.

Ludwig was driving near a park. Though the speed limit was 25, he was going 45. After he rounded a corner, Viola, a child who had been playing in the park, fell into the street. Ludwig saw Viola in time to avoid hitting her, and also noticed that Viola was looking up in horror as Ludwig's car approached. Still, Ludwig believed Viola would get out of the way in time, so he did not take evasive measures to avoid hitting her. By the time Ludwig realized that Viola was frozen with fear and unable to move, it was too late, and he struck her, inflicting serious injuries. Viola sues Ludwig for battery.

225. Which of the following statements is most accurate?

(A) Because Ludwig knew he would strike Viola if she did not move out of the way, also knew that Viola saw his car approaching, and struck her when she did not move, Ludwig will be liable.

(B) Because Ludwig should have known the grave risk of striking a child if he drove at such a high speed near a park, Ludwig will be liable.

(C) Because Ludwig intentionally violated a statute designed to protect a class of persons that included Viola, Ludwig will be liable.

(D) Because Ludwig did not possess the required intent, Ludwig will not be liable.

226. Give an example of overlap between invasion of privacy and intentional infliction of emotional distress.

ANSWER:

A mother named Ambrosia was at home one evening when she overheard a telephone conversation in which her son discussed his plan to kill a certain person who he believed had wronged him. Ambrosia did nothing, and the killing took place as planned.

227. If the victim's estate sues Ambrosia for wrongful death, which of the following statements is most likely correct?

(A) Ambrosia cannot be held liable because her failure to notify potential victims or the authorities was not a cause in fact of the murder.

(B) Ambrosia cannot be held liable because she has no duty to control the actions of others.

(C) Ambrosia cannot be held liable because the criminal conduct of her son and the others was a superseding cause of the victim's death.

(D) Ambrosia can be held liable.

Some critics of contemporary products liability law say that courts are too eager to hold defendants liable for failure to warn. When an unfortunate accident has injured the plaintiff, it is too tempting — and wrong, say the critics — to conclude that a warning would have prevented the injury.

228. Give arguments in support of this criticism, and then critique the criticism with counterarguments.
ANSWER:

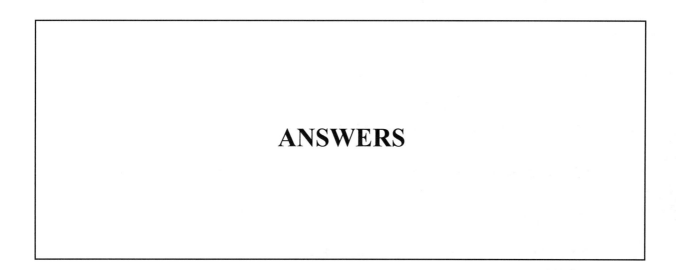

ANSWERS

1.   **Answer (B) is correct.** Battery requires an unlawful harmful or offensive touching. If Lecter had passed along the virus through contact with Starling, that would constitute a harmful touching. In addition, it would be unlawful because it is wrong for a person to infect another with a disease by means of intentionally touching another person. But here, although Lecter did touch Starling, he only did so as part of a surgery to which she had consented. To the extent her consent was not fully informed, courts tend to treat the matter as one for the law of negligence, not the law of battery. (Courts distinguish between uninformed "consent" and unconsented contact.)

      Answer (A) is incorrect because the mere fact that Starling consented to surgery does not resolve the problem. Had Lecter passed along the virus, Starling's consent to surgery would not defeat her battery claim against him.

      Answer (C) is incorrect because, while it is true that Lecter has privacy rights, those rights do not trump Starling's entitlement to freedom from harmful or offensive contact. Had the contact been harmful, she would have a valid battery claim.

      Answer (D) is incorrect because, as noted above, courts treat informed consent cases under the law of negligence rather than that of battery. (Of course, sometimes the line between less-than-fully-informed consent and unconsented contact is rather thin; in these cases, either claim might be viable.)

2.   **Answer (C) is correct.** A person who forms the intent to contact and carries out the contact is liable for battery, if the contact is unlawful. Even if the person suffers from an illness that makes her delusional or affects her ability to recognize the impropriety of her conduct, she is liable. Here, Marshall intended to strike Herrle. It is inappropriate to strike a nurse's aide in this way. Marshall is liable for battery.

      Answer (A) is incorrect because it provides only a policy reason for holding a person suffering from mental illness liable for battery. Marshall cannot be held liable, however, unless she harbors the necessary intent.

      Answer (B) is incorrect because a person must commit an "act," which in tort law means a volitional movement. If she did not control her arm's movement, Marshall did not commit an act. (On the facts here, she did "act.")

      Answer (D) is incorrect because the law of intentional torts does not base liability on the defendant's moral shortcomings. If she intended to commit a contact, that is sufficient (assuming the contact occurred and it is one that society deems unlawful).

3.   Yes, she can. Liability for assault turns on the (reasonable) understandings and perceptions of a plaintiff. If the defendant has acted in a way that indicates her capacity for inflicting imminent harmful contact, then the plaintiff who apprehends this contact can bring a claim for assault. For example, pointing an unloaded pistol at the plaintiff and pulling the trigger will typically suffice for assault liability, even if the pistol is unloaded. Lunging at the plaintiff while shouting a threat will also suffice, even if the defendant knows that she is weak and will collapse before she can reach the plaintiff's body.

4.   **Answer (B) is correct.** A jury is likely to find that, although Sam impliedly consented to being "tagged" in the game, he did not consent to being slugged. True, Rebecca did not mean to hurt Sam, but most courts do not require this in order to make out a battery claim.

     Answer (A) is incorrect because Rebecca was not exercising her right of self-defense. That is not the way the game of "tag" works. One seeks to avoid any contact with the person who is "it."

     Answer (C) is incorrect because, as indicated above, a jury is likely to find that Sam consented to light touches, not being slugged.

     Answer (D) is incorrect because most courts hold that a defendant in a battery case need not intend injury; it is sufficient if she intended a contact that the law deems inappropriate under the circumstances.

5.   **Answer (D) is correct.** Chloe's best argument is that a 10-year-old child is privileged to commit this kind of touching while on the playground. The argument might not prevail, but it is at least fairly viable. Society tolerates certain intentional contacts by children that it will not tolerate among adults.

     Answer (A) is incorrect because a person liable for battery pays for unintended consequences as well as intended consequences. There is some limit, of course, but that limit is not reached when a person shoved lightly falls and suffers an injury. If this was a battery, Chloe is liable for all the harm Karl suffered.

     Answer (B) is incorrect because a child of 10 can, indeed, form the intent to make harmful contact.

     Answer (C) is incorrect because, depending on the circumstances, even a gentle push can be a battery. If, for example, defendant gently pushes a person who is standing on the edge of a cliff, that push can constitute a battery.

6.   **Answer (B) is correct.** Intentional, offensive touching can suffice for battery liability, and unconsented-to operations have been held to satisfy the contact requirement. Because Sharon did not apprehend the touching before it happened, she would have no claim for assault.

Answer (A) is incorrect because Dr. Doolittle's touching of Letitia is privileged as emergency medical treatment.

Answer (C) illustrates an assault without a battery. Patrick was able to avoid harmful contact. Dr. Proctor's behavior satisfies the elements of assault.

Answer (D) is incorrect because Cankersore was aware of the touchings as they became imminent. If the battery claim is good, then the assault claim is equally good.

7. Intent refers to the actor's endeavor to use a particular means to effect a result. Motive refers to the actor's goals, desires, or emotions. Intent is narrower than motive, and it is intent, not motive, that the plaintiff must show in order to sustain liability for an intentional tort. So, for instance, an actor could have an admirable motive (for example, she wishes to disable a heinous dictator and thereby rescue thousands of innocents) at the same time that she fulfills the intent requirement for liability.

8. **Answer (A) is correct.** Although decisional law on the point is fairly rare, children younger than three have been held liable for battery. To satisfy the intent element, courts look to child's behavior. Typically when they find a child liable for battery they infer the child desired to inflict harmful contact — for example, by biting a playmate.

    Answer (B) is incorrect because a defendant need not be capable of verbal testimony in order to be held liable. Non-speaking defendants (e.g., mental incompetents, dead people) have been held liable.

    Answer (C) is incorrect because the ability to frame intent to inflict harmful contact is understood to take place at an earlier age than the ability to be negligent. The two types of tortious conduct have different age standards.

    Answer (D) is incorrect because even incompetents, such as the mentally disabled, can be liable in tort.

9. **Answer (A) is correct.** There are two ways for an actor to fulfill the intent requirement of battery: either purpose (or motive, or desire) or substantial certainty. If the element of purpose is present, substantial certainty need not be present.

    Answer (B) is incorrect because Siobhan did not act with substantial certainty. She was doubtful of her ability to carry out her plan.

    Answer (C) is incorrect because although substantial certainty was not present, purpose was present, and that suffices.

    Answer (D) is incorrect because even though the contact took place somewhat indirectly, Siobhan's actions set in motion a force that resulted in harmful contact.

10.   Both fear and apprehension take place from the perspective of the target, or plaintiff. Apprehension refers to anticipation: the plaintiff expects harmful contact. Fear refers to the way he feels about such contact. Fear is narrower than apprehension; in assault cases every feared contact is an apprehended contact, but not every apprehended contact is a feared contact. A plaintiff might apprehend, but not fear, an instance of imminent harmful contact for several reasons: he might be strong enough to withstand pain or laugh it off; he might have faith that no harm can befall him; he might rate himself as stronger or more dangerous than the assailant.

11.   **Answer (A) is correct.** The issue here is the lawfulness of Robert's confinement. If Southwood was following statutorily established procedures, it is difficult to argue that its behavior was inappropriate.

      Answer (B) is incorrect because it misconstrues the facts. Southwood *did* intend to confine Robert because it meant to keep him in the facility.

      Answer (C) is incorrect because physical restraint is not a prerequisite for confinement. Preventing a person from leaving a building can constitute confinement, even if force is not used.

      Answer (D) is incorrect because, as indicated above, Robert was restricted to the building and not permitted to leave. This is confinement.

12.   **Answer (C) is correct.** Frank bought a ticket to a particular destination, as did the other passengers. Though one can understand Frank's anxiety after the engine blowout and his desire to land at a closer airport, there was, in fact, no need to divert the plane. Thus, the airline's refusal, which kept Frank confined for longer than he wanted to be, was not unlawful.

      Answer (A) is incorrect because there *was* confinement. As explained above, it was not unlawful, but Frank was certainly confined.

      Answer (B) is incorrect because it makes no sense. The other passengers would not be falsely imprisoned by landing at a closer airport. In fact, their confinement on the plane would end sooner than if they proceeded to the original destination.

      Answer (D) is incorrect because physical harm is not an element of false imprisonment, as long as the victim knows of the confinement (and Frank is well aware of it in this situation).

13.   **Answer (C) is correct.** An action for false imprisonment requires intentional confinement. Although a defendant often takes more direct measures to confine the plaintiff, wrongful withholding of property can fulfill the element of confinement. Because Grudgepudge would forfeit his laptop if he left Sam's office without it, and because Sam had no good reason to take Grudgepudge's laptop, Sam has fulfilled the elements of this intentional tort.

      Answer (A) is incorrect because Sam had no privilege to possess the laptop.

      Answer (B) is incorrect because, as was stated above, the wrongful withholding of property can amount to confinement.

Answer (D) is the least incorrect of the three incorrect choices, but it does not explain the outcome in terms of Sam's intentional behavior; moreover, "reasonable compulsion to remain" is not an element of false imprisonment.

14.   **Answer (A) is correct.** Although an omission can sometimes be the basis of liability for false imprisonment — for example, when a jailer refuses to release a prison inmate after getting lawful orders to do so, the jailer might be liable to the inmate — the defendant must have owed the plaintiff a duty. Pia and Rhonda were strangers and the facts give no basis for imposing a duty to rescue on this "passerby." Thus Pia did not imprison Rhonda.

       Answer (B) is incorrect because more than one individual can be liable in tort for the same consequences. Tort law does not recognize the concept of one solitary "proper defendant" for each injury.

       Answer (C) is incorrect because voluntary entry into a space does not preclude liability for false imprisonment thereafter.

       Answer (D) is incorrect because the facts do not establish that Rhonda was a trespasser; and, in any event, the condition of being a trespasser does not, of itself, defeat a claim for false imprisonment.

15.   In most jurisdictions, through statutes or case law, Escamillo has a limited privilege to protect the store against shoplifting using reasonable detention. The facts suggest that the privilege would have force here. Escamillo may intercept Gretchen on her way out the door and detain her — that is, tell her that she may not leave for a limited period of time while he investigates. The privilege has requirements. First, Escamillo must have a reasonable belief that Gretchen is in the middle of committing theft. This requirement appears to be fulfilled. Second, the detention must take place in a reasonable manner. If Gretchen resists detention, Escamillo may not use deadly force to detain her. Third, the detention must take place for only a reasonable period of time, and this time must be used for investigation.

16.   **Answer (B) is correct.** False imprisonment is one of the intentional torts that are covered by the doctrine of transferred intent. Under transferred intent, a defendant may be liable for the consequences of one intentional tort when he acted intentionally to fulfill the elements of another tort. Hommyside intended to kill Hurley (consequence: battery) and his behavior caused her to be confined (consequence: false imprisonment).

       Answer (A) is incorrect because "physical barrier" usually refers to a more direct physical obstacle, such as a locked door. Answer (A) also omits reference to Hommyside's mental state, a crucial element of any intentional tort.

       Answer (C) is incorrect because under the doctrine of transferred intent, an actor can intend one set of consequences and be liable for another.

Answer (D) is incorrect because voluntary entry into a space does not preclude liability for false imprisonment thereafter. Moreover, assumption of risk typically applies to accidental harms, not intentional ones.

17. **Answer (A) is correct.** Although Klutzmonkey's behavior might be the basis of liability using another tort theory — strict liability or nuisance, perhaps — trespass to land usually requires that something tangible or visible enter the other's land. Sound waves do not fulfill this criterion.

    Answer (B) is incorrect because Yodel has fulfilled the elements of trespass to land. He has acted intentionally with the desire to create an invasion, and the neighbor's land was invaded.

    Answer (C) is incorrect because invasions just above the lateral surface of the earth are sufficiently low to constitute trespass. (Jet airplanes flying thousands of feet in the air are not low enough.)

    Answer (D) is incorrect because the failure to remove a physical object once privileged to be there, but no longer privileged, constitutes a trespass.

18. Gallant has fulfilled the elements of trespass to land. He intentionally entered the land of another. The facts indicate that he had no privilege to do so. Damage is presumed, even though Gallant did not harm Landholder's land. Token damages ("a dollar") may be in order. Mordred has fulfilled what many courts call "negligent trespass to land." His careless driving caused him to enter Landholder's land, even though he did not intend to do so. For negligent trespass to land, courts do not presume damages, and so Mordred would not be liable to Landholder. If he had done some harm to the land–for example, damaged a flower garden–then Mordred would be liable for the harm his negligent invasion caused.

19. **Answer (C) is correct.** Trespass to chattels, unlike trespass to land, usually requires actual damages. There are two kinds of trespass to chattels — "intermeddling," where the defendant does harm to the chattel, and "dispossession," where the defendant does something to interfere with the plaintiff's right of possession. Francine's behavior would fall within the "intermeddling" category. Were there no "World's Greatest Clunker" competition, Cindy would probably have no remedy against Francine. But because the computer might well have been a prizewinner in its original state, Francine has harmed the chattel.

    Answer (A) is incorrect because the roommate is not a possessor of the chattel and so her consent to the intermeddling is of no significance.

    Answer (B) is incorrect because under the facts Cindy experienced detriment as well as benefit from the intermeddling.

    Answer (D) is incorrect because the roommate had authority to admit a visitor to her dormitory room. The injury is to a chattel, not to the possession of land.

20.   **Answer (B) is correct.** Conversion is an intentional tort, based on the defendant's intent to perform an act that interferes with a plaintiff's right of possession. Intentional alteration of a chattel — for example, spray-painting it with graffiti — would constitute conversion (if the alteration is severe enough to warrant that the defendant pay full value of the chattel). Negligent alteration is merely negligence.

       Answer (A) is incorrect because wrongful transfer — for example, using someone else's chattel as collateral for a loan and then having the chattel seized by the creditor–can constitute conversion.

       Answer (C) is incorrect because theft — the crime of taking something that isn't yours with the intent of depriving the owner of possessionfulfills the elements of conversion.

       Answer (D) is incorrect because even a good-faith purchaser can be a converter if the chattel was stolen from the true owner.

21.   The tort of conversion applies to tangible physical property that can be moved, as well as to documents in which title to a chattel is merged, such as a bill of lading, and documents that convey the value of a tangible chattel, such as a promissory note. The tort is intended to cover that which can be quickly alienated. Real property is not included. Neither is intellectual property. Intangible assets, such as the goodwill or trade secrets of a business, are also not included.

22.   **Answer (C) is correct.** When a person is unaware of his confinement during the time he is confined, he may only recover for false imprisonment if he suffered physical injury as a result of the confinement. Because Peter did not learn of his confinement until after it had ended, and because he was not physically injured by the confinement, he may not recover for false imprisonment.

       Answer (A) is incorrect because actual confinement is not sufficient.

       Answer (B) is incorrect because, even if the emotional effects of learning of the confinement are severe, the plaintiff who was unaware of the confinement while it was occurring may not recover for false imprisonment unless the plaintiff was physically injured.

       Answer (D) is incorrect because false imprisonment is a "trespassory tort," and intent to confine one person will "transfer" to the person actually confined. Thus, it does not matter that the manager intended to confine a different person.

23.   **Answer (D) is correct.** Dougray intended to confine Penny. She was, in fact, confined to her store. Though she could have used the fire escape to leave, a jury might well find that it was not unreasonable for her to fail to use a fire escape from the 10th floor. (Many people are afraid of heights, and fire escapes are a good deal more daunting than simple stair-

ways.) It does not matter that Penny was rescued after only an hour; during that hour, she was confined.

Answer (A) is incorrect because confinement for an hour is long enough.

Answer (B) is incorrect because, as explained above, a jury might well find that the fire escape was not a reasonable means of escape.

Answer (C) is incorrect because Penny did suffer cognizable harm: her wrongful confinement for a period of time.

24.   **Answer (A) is correct.** Denny put Potter in the position of choosing between leaving without his wallet and staying in the car. He had no right to impose this no-win option. Potter was not truly free to leave, as doing so would have required him to give up both his car and his wallet. Thus, he was, in a real sense, confined.

Answer (B) is incorrect for the reason just given. Potter did not really have a free choice.

Answers (C) and (D) are incorrect because the existence of other possible causes of action does not deny access to the false imprisonment claim. The same facts can give rise to several claims.

25.   In most U.S. courts, Pasha would not have a valid claim. The paradigm for false imprisonment generally followed is one of "confinement" within bounds set by the defendant. Under that concept, Pasha was not falsely imprisoned because she was free to go anywhere she wanted except by one specific route. A different paradigm would recognize an unlawful restriction on one's freedom to travel as false imprisonment; and, indeed, that is what happened in this case. But most courts have not adopted that concept.

26. **Answer (B) is correct.** Normally, words that negate a party's aggressive actions make the actions non-tortious. But this is not a categorical rule. In some situations, it is perfectly reasonable for a victim to believe that despite the aggressor's words to the contrary, the aggressor is going to strike her. It is also permissible for the jury to infer that the aggressor intends the victim to have that belief. A jury question exists in such cases, and this appears to be that type of case.

   Answer (A) is incorrect because, as indicated above, the defendant's choice of words that negate her actions does not always make the conduct benign.

   Answer (C) is incorrect because the tort of assault not only violates one's interest in freedom from harmful contact. It also violates one's interests in freedom from offensive contact. If the jury concludes that Emily's punch was not an excessively violent means of terminating the attack, Emily will have acted in reasonable self-defense, and will not be liable.

   Answer (D) is incorrect because, as indicated above, sometimes it is reasonable to harm a person to prevent an attack.

27. As a general rule, yes. A defendant should not be allowed to escape liability simply because he or she successfully defrauded the plaintiff. Courts do, however, distinguish between "fraud in fact" or "fraud as to an essential matter" on the one hand, and "fraud as to a collateral matter" on the other. For example, if the plaintiff agreed to what would otherwise have been a battery in exchange for a payment of money, and the payment turns out to be counterfeit money or a bad check, then the consent to the harmful contact is valid. The plaintiff cannot recover for the harmful contact (and will have to try to get paid by some other means, such as a contract action or a private right of action based on violation of the criminal law or consumer law).

28. **Answer (A) is correct.** Most courts would hold that a person is entitled to use self-defense if she reasonably believes she is under attack by another. Thus, even a mistaken belief can justify self-defense.

   Answer (B) is incorrect because the facts do not suggest temporary insanity. And, even if George was temporarily insane, that begs the question whether his reaction was reasonable under the circumstances.

   Answer (C) is incorrect because George's reaction was volitional. The facts make clear that he meant to do what he did. That makes it a volitional act.

Answer (D) is incorrect because the facts show that George was not deprived of the ability to control his movements. On the contrary, he meant to do exactly what he did.

29.   The privilege of public necessity permits an actor to interfere with the property of another person in order to avoid a threatened harm of greater magnitude to the public good. Usually this threat comes from a natural force, like a flood or an earthquake. For instance, if a person's property stands near a raging wildfire, and this property is likely to make the disaster worse if it is not destroyed (it could augment the size of the fire), an actor is privileged to destroy the property. Other examples: killing the plaintiff's rabid dog, removing the plaintiff's car parked at a fire hydrant in order to extinguish a fire.

"The public good" refers to some collective of persons, such as the residents of a village, although this "public" can be relatively small in size — for example, the occupants of a ferry about to sink if its cargo is not jettisoned (*see* Mouse's Case, 77 Eng. Rep. 1341 (K.B. 1609)). The privilege is absolute, meaning that the actor pays no compensation to the person whose property is destroyed. Because of the unfairness of making one private property holder pay for a communal good, whose beneficiaries are not paying for this destruction yet receive a benefit, legislation often does what tort law will not do, and compensates the property holder by statute. *See, e.g.,* 21 U.S.C. § 114a (providing compensation to owners of cattle that have been killed in order to prevent the spread of hoof-and-mouth disease).

30.   **Answer (B) is correct.** Jane expressly "invites," or challenges, Ralph to commit what would otherwise be a battery (the intentional infliction of harmful bodily contact).

Answer (A) is incorrect because Victor did not consent to harmful bodily contact. Under these facts, he might have consented to false imprisonment.

Answer (C) is incorrect because Dilbert's raising of his arm constitutes at most implied consent, not express consent.

Answer (D) is incorrect because, as is the case with answer (C), there is no express consent, merely acquiescence in a longstanding trespass.

31.   Rupert has a claim against Hannah, and Hannah has a claim against Rupert, for battery. Battery is the intentional infliction of harmful contact. Each of these two individuals "pounded at" the other in this fistfight that began as a discussion of professional sports, indicating that the blows were intentional acts. Hannah and Rupert both desired to inflict harmful contact on the other, and harmful contact resulted from their actions. Jurisdictions differ on whether their consent to the blows will bar their claims. The fistfight appears to have been consensual. The majority rule is that consent to an illegal act is ineffective. The *Restatement (Second) of Torts* and some jurisdictions disagree, holding that consent to a criminal act is a valid defense in an action for an intentional tort. If the jurisdiction follows the majority rule, the status of the fistfight as a criminal breach of the peace would make the consent ineffective, and so Rupert and Hannah would each have a battery claim against the other.

32. **Answer (D) is correct.** "Consent implied by law" is a kind of implied consent where the plaintiff did not, in fact, imply that he or she consented to an action. Instead the law infers that a reasonable person would, in that circumstance, accept this behavior. The doctrine is used where a plaintiff is unable to give or withhold consent. Here, it seems fair to infer that Dauphine needed some kind of touching in order to be rescued; she could not say yes or no at the time, and Pallowag's touching does not exceed these bounds.

Answer (A) is incorrect because to the extent any consent is implied, it is implied in fact — or, in other words, by Adam himself — rather than by law.

Answer (B) is incorrect for similar reasons. Belinda consented in fact. (She may not have given "informed consent," but that is another matter.)

Answer (C) is incorrect because the doctrine of consent implied by law, in the medical context, applies only to emergencies or other unusual circumstances where the plaintiff cannot be asked what he or she wishes. This scenario depicts a physician who deviates from a patient's consent.

33. **Answer (B) is correct.** The privilege to inflict deadly force on another arises when a person reasonably believes that such deadly force is necessary in order to fend off an attack. When it appears that a burglar is holding a firearm, a homeowner or other person in possession of a home is privileged to defend himself or herself through deadly force. This person has no duty to retreat inside the home.

Answer (A) is incorrect because Joplin had no duty to retreat.

Answer (C) is incorrect because Joplin had the mental state to sustain a prima facie claim of battery by Rugrat. The claim is defeated by Joplin's privilege of self-defense.

Answer (D) is incorrect because there is no such status in tort law as a "criminal trespasser." Moreover, Rugrat's entering another person's home in order to commit a crime is not the reason that his battery claim fails. The privilege turns on Joplin's reasonable beliefs, not Rugrat's reasons for being there.

34. **Answer (A) is correct.** (Facetious answers about improving the world by killing off the lower orders are incorrect.) One key problem with spring guns and other indiscriminate property-protecting devices is that they do not know whom they injure. Some intruders are present for innocent reasons. Another problem with these devices is that they can hurt not only intruders but inhabitants. Accordingly, a "good" place to use a spring gun, if there is such a place, is a remote location where inhabitants won't get hurt and where protection by human beings (police officers, private security personnel) is unavailing for some reason. Answer (A) best fits this description.

Answer (B) is incorrect because the spring gun is likely to hurt the inhabitants.

Answer (C) is incorrect because security personnel are much less indiscriminate than spring guns, and can keep unnecessary wounding (or killing) to a minimum.

Answer (D) is incorrect for many reasons. One of them is that setting up a spring gun presumes a sharp distinction between intruders and inhabitants — but in this house they are more or less the same people. Shooting randomly at drug sellers, users, and customers is a bad solution to the social problems that these persons manifest and cause.

35.   You could be wrong, but it looks as if the person about to drink has been given a dangerous substance without her consent. Your privilege to use force in her defense extends to what is reasonable under the circumstances. Knocking the drink out of her hand onto the floor would be reasonable, and you'd have a privilege in an action by the person about to drink, should she bring a claim for battery, or by the bar, for trespass to their chattel. Brawling with the maybe-assailant would go beyond the needs of defense.

36.   **Answer (C) is correct.** This question involves an issue of affirmative duty. In the absence of such a duty, Eve cannot be held liable to Adam. Friends do not fit within a traditional "special relationship," but some courts have held that friends on a mutually beneficial joint venture do have an affirmative duty to protect each other. *See, e.g.*, Farwell v. Keaton, 240 N.W.2d 217 (Mich. 1976). Adam's best argument here would be to assert that he and Eve were on such a venture.

   Answer (A) is incorrect because, although it was improper for Adam and Eve to scale the fence on the construction site (they were trespassers), it was not the act of going there that in itself caused harm to Adam and for which he seeks to hold Eve responsible. It was her failure to render assistance to him after he was injured.

   Answer (B) is incorrect because vicarious liability does not apply to this situation. Adam was not Eve's agent. To be held liable, Eve must have been negligent, meaning that she either committed an act of misfeasance or failed unreasonably to help Adam when she had a duty to do so.

   Answer (D) is incorrect because it is not enough to say that failure to assist was the cause in fact and proximate cause of harm. The traditional no-duty-to-rescue rule is not based on considerations of causation or proximate cause. It is a policy-based rule that applies even when a party is the cause in fact and proximate cause of another party's harm.

37.   **Answer (B) is correct.** Sara had no duty to assist Adam, but if she chose to do so, she was obligated to exercise reasonable care in her undertaking. It will be a jury question whether, under the circumstances, it was unreasonable for Sara to attempt to convey Adam to the hospital if her vehicle was very low on gasoline.

   Answer (A) is incorrect because it assumes Sara would be strictly liable once she undertook to assist Adam. Her duty, once assumed by Sara, is only that of a reasonable person.

   Answer (C) is incorrect because it assumes one may not be found negligent when acting under emergency circumstances. The law provides that the jury may take the emergency into account as one factor in determining whether the party acted reasonably. It is possible to act unreasonably even under emergency circumstances.

   Answer (D) is incorrect because it assumes "Good Samaritan" statutes protect all rescuers except those whose conduct constitutes intentional wrongdoing. In fact, the protections of these statutes is more narrow; they tend only to protect rescuers whose conduct is merely negligent. Rescuers whose conduct constitutes something worse than negligence, such as recklessness, "willful or wanton" misconduct, or intentional misconduct, are typically excluded from the protection of the statutes. In addition, some statutes only protect medical professionals.

38.   An unforeseeable plaintiff is a plaintiff whose claim arises based on the negligence of a defendant with respect to a *different* plaintiff. The famous story of Palsgraf v. Long Island R.R. Co., 248 N.Y. 339, 162 N.E. 99 (1928) provides an illustration. According to the Cardozo opinion, railroad employees negligently pushed and pulled a passenger onto a departing train, causing the passenger's package (which did not appear dangerous) to fall from his arms and explode. This negligence, Cardozo held, created liability only to a small set of potential plaintiffs. Palsgraf was standing at some distance from the push and suffered injury from the explosion. According to the Cardozo rationale, Palsgraf was an unforesee-able plaintiff. The risk of injury to her was outside of what a reasonable person in the position of defendant's employees would have foreseen.

39.   **Answer (B) is correct.** Most likely, the koi pond qualifies as an "attractive nuisance" because it is reasonably foreseeable that it will attract young children who will not appreciate the dangers and who, because of their age, are unlikely to be able to protect themselves from those dangers. (Note that many disfavor this term — be careful if you choose to use it.) It is also likely that Peter is aware of this danger. If the pond qualifies as an attractive nuisance, Peter has a duty of reasonable care to protect children from the dangers posed by the pond. In this situation, Peter has a very strong argument that he has satisfied that duty. An eight-foot chain link fence certainly will keep out all but the most persistent children, and the facts indicate that Stewie was "particularly agile." Thus, though Peter probably owed Stewie a duty of reasonable care, Peter most likely satisfied that duty.

        Answer (A) is incorrect because it fails to acknowledge the likelihood that the koi pond qualifies as an attractive nuisance.

        Answer (C) is incorrect because visibility for the sidewalk is only one part of the test for establishing the koi pond as an attractive nuisance. Stewie may not recover solely for the reason that the pond was visible from the sidewalk.

        Answer (D) is incorrect for the same type of reason as answer (C). Though inability to appreciate the danger posed by the koi pond is one prerequisite to categorizing the pond as an attractive nuisance, it is not sufficient in itself.

40.   **Answer (C) is correct.** *Restatement (Second) of Torts* § 322 (1965) provides that one who causes harm, even non-negligently, has a duty to exercise reasonable care to assist the injured person. Yancey was not a tortfeasor, but was a causal factor in Horton's injury. This imposed on Yancey a duty to use reasonable care to assist Horton. Because Yancey failed to assist, and because Horton suffered further harm as a result of the delay in receiving treatment, Yancey will be liable for these additional damages.

Answer (A) is incorrect for the reason just given: Yancey has a duty even though he was not at fault in the accident.

Answer (B) is incorrect because Yancey's duty is not secondary to Quint's. Both Quint and Yancey have a duty of reasonable care.

Answer (D) is incorrect because the liability of Yancey will be limited to the additional harm Horton suffered as a result of the delay in treatment. Yancey was not at fault in the original accident.

41. **Answer (B) is correct.** Though Bobby was not in the store to conduct any business, he was accompanying Hank, who was there for such a purpose and was therefore an invitee. Under the circumstances, it is unlikely that Hank could have done his shopping without taking the kid along, so in a sense, his presence in the store was necessary to Hank's carrying out of business there. Thus, Bobby was also an invitee, to whom a duty of reasonable care was owed. Because a question of material fact remains about whether Arlene's exercised reasonable care in maintaining its display of power saws, summary judgment is not appropriate.

Answer (A) is incorrect because, as explained above, Bobby was an invitee.

Answer (C) is incorrect because Bobby was not a licensee.

Answer (D) is incorrect because even if Hank negligently supervised Bobby, his negligence would not be imputed to Bobby so as to defeat Bobby's claim against Arlene's.

42. **Answer (D) is correct.** A physician has an ethical duty to assist a person in need of medical attention, but does not have a legal duty unless the physician caused the need for medical attention or has a special relationship with the person. Neither is true here. The physician's failure to act is reprehensible, but not tortious.

Answer (A) is incorrect because merely having the ability to assist does not impose an obligation to do so.

Answer (B) is incorrect because sharing the status of passengers on a commercial flight does not create a special relationship among them. In some sense, they are all "in it together," but this is more a matter of coincidence than any voluntary association. Perhaps if the plane had made a hard landing and the survivors were stranded while awaiting assistance, a court would find that their relationship was one of dependence on each other. But that is not the case here.

Answer (C) is incorrect because, as explained above, the passengers were not in a special relationship with each other. In addition, as also explained above, the physician's ability to assist does not impose a legal obligation to assist.

43. **Answer (B) is correct.** The firefighter's rule provides that a public employee who suffers an injury caused by a kind of hazard that she confronts as a normal part of her job does not have a negligence claim against the person who created the hazard. Pursuing suspects is part of Krumpke's job as a police officer. He may not sue Willie for negligence.

Answer (A) is incorrect because it fails to take account of the firefighter's rule.

Answer (C) is incorrect because Willie had no duty to protect Krumpke from this hazard.

Answer (D) is incorrect because the facts do not make clear that Krumpke actually failed to exercise reasonable care. The opposite is probably true; the facts state that Krumpke could tell that the stairway was rotted, but tried to avoid the weak spots. Under the emergency circumstances in which he found himself, Krumpke probably exercised reasonable care. In addition, the court will not need to reach this issue because, as discussed above, the firefighter's rule will prevent Krumpke from recovering for Willie's negligence.

44. Imposing a general duty to exercise reasonable care through both affirmative conduct and failure to act, or eliminating "duty" from the prima facie case, would make many more claims actionable, with unfortunate results. Claims alleging economic and emotional injury would be much harder to dispose of before trial. Liability for omissions would expand: without limited duty, an obligation to prevent harm by others or to eliminate suffering unrelated to tortious conduct would foster new claims.

45. The driver could argue that she had a duty only to "persons" in the vehicle, and the fetus is not a person because its existence hinges on the wishes of its mother; "persons" do not have this kind of dependent, contingent existence. Courts reject this reasoning. They see a fetus (in some states, only a viable fetus) as a holder of rights against tortfeasors, the abortion rights of pregnant women notwithstanding. The prerogative of a woman to end her pregnancy does not mean that strangers can also end it, or harm a fetus, without legal consequences.

46.   **Answer (D) is correct.** A reasonably foreseeable risk of failing to dim one's high beams when an oncoming driver approaches is that the driver will be blinded momentarily. This, in turn, creates a risk of colliding with another vehicle, a pedestrian, an animal, or another object on or near the road. This is exactly what happened in this case. As long as the moose was not on the street because of any negligence on Carla's part (and the facts suggest that this was true), its owner (Carla) may recover its value.

        Answer (A) is incorrect because, even if keeping the moose was dangerous, that fact is irrelevant to the question of Rebecca's liability to Carla for her own negligence.

        Answer (B) is incorrect because imposing liability on Rebecca for the loss of the moose is not double liability. Her payment to Norm was for Norm's damages, not Carla's.

        Answer (C) is incorrect because liability does not depend on a judgment that a reasonable person would foresee the precise circumstances of an accident; it is sufficient if a reasonable person would foresee the possible classes of victims and the general type of harm that might occur as a result of the negligent behavior. As explained above, physical harm to an animal is a reasonably foreseeable consequence of Rebecca's careless act. As a result, Rebecca can be held liable to Carla for the loss of the moose.

47.   **Answer (D) is correct.** Res ipsa loquitur does not apply unless plaintiff shows that this is the type of event that does not normally occur in the absence of negligence. Many things can explain the bacterial contamination of the water supply, and only some of the explanations involve negligence. Perhaps plaintiff could have called an expert witness to lay the foundation for the finding that negligence probably explains the accident, but the facts as given do not state that plaintiff called an expert. Moreover, if there was negligence, it must have been defendant's negligence that caused the event. (Often, this is stated as the requirement that the negligent act occurred when the instrumentality of the event was in the "exclusive control" of the defendant.) From these sketchy facts, there is no way to tell when the contamination occurred.

        Answer (A) is incorrect because, as stated above, plaintiff has not shown that this is the type of accident normally caused by negligence. This would be mere speculation.

        Answer (B) is incorrect because it does not state the "type of accident" requirement in the usual way. There is, in fact, a difference between asking whether this is the type of accident that is usually caused by negligence, and saying that this is the type of accident that doesn't normally occur if due care is used. The latter formulation is much easier to satisfy than the former, and the former is the more commonly used.

Answer (C) is incorrect because no facts are presented that would show that the contamination occurred when defendant was in exclusive control of the water supply. Plaintiff has not offered any evidence to show when the water became contaminated, or by what instrumentality. To reach the conclusion that it happened when the water was under defendant's control would be speculation, not a rational, "more likely than not" inference from the known facts.

48. The difference lies in how much freedom the factfinder (jury or judge) has to deem the defendant to have been *not* negligent. Under "negligence per se," violation of a relevant statute establishes duty and breach as a matter of law. The defendant is deemed negligent for having violated the statute and caused injury to the plaintiff thereby. Under the "evidence of negligence" approach, violation of the statute is relevant to establish negligence, but not dispositive. The factfinder can reject this evidence and deem the defendant not negligent.

49. **Answer (A) is correct.** According to Learned Hand's formula, the likelihood of harm and its degree need to be balanced against the burden of avoiding the harm. In this case, avoiding the harm would mean granting fewer, or no, furloughs. This, in turn, might impede recovery, imposing greater costs on society to keep people institutionalized who otherwise would have been sufficiently recovered to be free. If the burden exceeds the discounted harm, Hospital should not be found negligent.

     Answer (B) is incorrect because custom is not the categorical (per se) measure of reasonable care. It is only evidence of what is reasonable.

     Answer (C) is incorrect because the harm to patients' recovery if the program is cancelled does not affect the causation factor in this case. It affects the duty/breach calculation.

     Answer (D) is incorrect because, as shown above, the evidence is relevant to the questions of duty and breach.

50. **Answer (A) is correct.** One of the statute's purposes was to protect the safety of cab passengers. Presumably, the legislature had in mind almost exactly the type of accident that occurred here: being struck by a vehicle traveling between the cab and the curb. It does not matter that the harm was immediately caused by a speeding bank robber rather than a lawfully driven vehicle preparing to make a right turn.

     Answer (B) is incorrect because, as explained above, George was harmed in the general type of accident the statute was designed to prevent.

     Answer (C) is incorrect because it is probably not true. If Jerry had stopped the cab closer to the curb, there would not have been room for Elaine to maneuver to the right of the cab. Thus, she would not have hit George.

Answer (D) is incorrect because it does not matter that the harm came about as a result of a criminal actor. As explained above, the harm was of the general type against which the statute was designed to protect cab passengers.

51.   **Answer (D) is correct.** Courts hold that customary violation of a safety statute does not overcome the statute's requirements. Violation is still negligence.

Answer (A) is incorrect because the custom to violate the statute does not affect the conclusion that the violator was negligent.

Answer (B) is incorrect because, absent information about the legislature's deliberations not given in the question, it is not reasonable to infer that the legislature meant to allow custom to trump the standard set forth in the statute. The contrary is almost certainly true.

Answer (C) is incorrect because what the "great mass" of bus and cab drivers do does not change the fact that it constitutes a violation of the statutory obligation to stop closer to the curb.

52.   **Answer (D) is correct.** Res ipsa loquitur applies when (1) this is the type of accident that is usually caused by negligence; (2) the instrumentality that caused the accident was in the exclusive control of the defendant; and (3) the plaintiff did not contribute meaningfully to the accident. Here, requirement (3) is clearly satisfied; Angela had nothing to do with the accident's occurrence. The real issue is whether there was probably negligence and whether any negligence was probably that of AmuseCo (whether the instrumentality was in AmuseCo's possession at the time of any negligence). It seems reasonable to infer as a matter of common sense and experience that a carousel does not normally accelerate too much unless there is negligence in its operation or maintenance. Though it would be better for Angela to offer expert testimony to establish this fact, most courts would probably hold that an expert is not absolutely required to get the case to the jury. And because the carousel was owned and operated by AmuseCo, it is highly likely that any negligent operation or maintenance was AmuseCo's responsibility.

Answer (A) is incorrect because a negligence case may be established purely through circumstantial evidence. Res ipsa loquitur does not operate only if there is direct evidence of negligence.

Answer (B) is incorrect because, as noted above, this is not a situation in which expert testimony is required to establish the first element of the res ipsa loquitur test.

Answer (C) is incorrect because a plaintiff is not required to eliminate all other possibilities in order to get a case to the jury based on circumstantial evidence. The court need only find that a reasonable jury could believe that, more likely than not, that there was negligence, and that defendant was the negligent party.

53. **Answer (C) is correct.** If the court decides that res ipsa loquitur applies, that only means that plaintiff has a strong enough case to reach the jury. It does *not* mean that plaintiff's claim must prevail in the absence of contrary evidence offered by defendant. Thus, application of the doctrine here means only that the court should deny Angela's motion and let the jury decide the case. (Note that in some unusual circumstances, plaintiff's circumstantial evidence might be so strong that it entitles plaintiff to a directed verdict in the absence of contrary evidence on the negligence issue. But that clearly is not the case here.)

     Answer (A) is incorrect because, as suggested above, defendant is not obligated to offer evidence of non-negligence. Though defendant might well want to do so, it need not do so.

     Answer (B) is incorrect because the evidence is not so strong as to mandate a verdict for Angela; it merely gets her to the jury.

     Answer (D) is incorrect because a party with better access to information does not typically risk an adverse directed verdict by declining to offer evidence. In some cases, the party does not have any additional evidence, and even if this is not true, the mere fact of greater access to evidence is not alone a reason to direct a verdict for the opponent.

54. **Answer (D) is correct.** Once again, there is still only a jury question. By offering evidence that someone else might have been responsible for the accident, AmuseCo has only given the jury something more to chew on. (In some cases, the party against whom the res ipsa doctrine has been invoked will offer such overwhelmingly strong evidence of non-negligence that the court should take the case from the jury by directing a verdict for that party. That is not the case here. The sight of another person tinkering with the apparatus and then running from the scene before the accident is fairly suggestive that someone else was responsible, but that does not entitle AmuseCo to a directed verdict. In fact, plaintiff might wish to argue that AmuseCo's security measures were inadequate, leaving the area open to tampering by outsiders.

     Answer (A) is incorrect for the reason just given. It is not so clear that AmuseCo was not negligent that the court should take the matter out of the jury's hands.

     Answer (B) is incorrect for similar reasons. The case is not so strong for Angela as to require a directed verdict in her favor. Though the evidence presented here can cut either way, its greater force is probably to make AmuseCo's negligence *harder*, not easier, to infer. Thus, a directed verdict for Angela is clearly not in order.

     Answer (C) is incorrect because there is sufficient evidence for the jury to make a rational decision on the negligence question. It would not be engaging in mere speculation.

55. **Answer (C) is correct.** Sam was engaged in a child's game. Some courts would also take note that the game was not a dangerous game (which is one reason it's considered a child-like activity). Most courts hold that the jury may consider the child's age in such cases when

deciding whether the child acted reasonably. One reason for the rule is to encourage children to learn from experience, which benefits them (and those around them) when they grow up.

Answer (A) is incorrect because children can be liable for negligence. There is no categorical rule in most jurisdictions forbidding that. Though some states use a "rule of 7" to immunize children under 7 for certain torts, that rule will not apply because Sam was 10.

Answer (B) is incorrect because even a child engaged in a child's activity can act negligently. This would be true if Sam did not exercise the care and skill that would be exercised by a reasonable person of roughly his age.

Answer (D) is incorrect because the game was not dangerous, at least not in the way activities normally deemed "adult" are dangerous.

56. **Answer (B) is correct.** Under this standard, the decision to become intoxicated can itself be negligence — particularly if the defendant does something risky, such as drive a car.

    Answer (A) is incorrect because it is too lenient: having become intoxicated as a matter of choice ("voluntarily"), the defendant should not benefit from a lower standard of care.

    Answer (C) is incorrect because negligence law does not recognize "the reasonable person with a mental deficiency" for a defendant.

    Answer (D) is incorrect, although it may look attractive for drunk driving and the like. Many instances of negligence, however, arise when the intoxicated defendant is violating no statute or otherwise warranting a finding of negligence per se (another way to say "negligent as a matter of law").

57. **Answer (C) is correct.** All the variables increase. A busy harbor is more likely to experience collisions than a quiet one; ships become more valuable and expensive in wartime; and wage labor becomes more expensive during wartime (able-bodied workers become occupied as soldiers).

    Answers (A), (B), and (D) are incorrect for the reasons stated.

58. **Answer (A) is correct.** According to the doctrine of negligence per se, a person who violates a statute designed to protect a class of persons that includes the plaintiff is deemed to have breached a duty of care toward the plaintiff if the harm that occurs is the type of harm the statute was designed to prevent. Here, all requirements seem to be satisfied. The statute limiting speed near the park to 25 miles per hour was almost certainly designed to protect children and others who might be near the park. The type of harm that occurred was a personal injury from being hit by a car. Golem breached his duty of care toward Ronnie.

Answer (B) is incorrect because it is almost certain that this was the type of injury the statute was designed to prevent. It is difficult to imagine what other type of injury the statute might have been aimed at preventing.

Answer (C) is incorrect because, under the traditional negligence per se doctrine, violation of a statute that meets the requirements set forth above does *not* present *some evidence* of negligence for the jury to consider. It *establishes* negligence (at least in the absence of a recognized excuse, none of which apply here).

Answer (D) is incorrect because, as long as safety is one purpose of the statute, it can qualify for application of the negligence per se doctrine.

59.   In furnishing medical services, the physician is held to the standards of a member of the medical profession in good standing. She is not held to the unmodified "reasonable person" standard, which would be too low. Jurisdictions divide over whether to compare the physician to a "national," "local," or "similar community" standard.

60.   The child is held to the standard of a child of similar age, intelligence, and experience. This treatment is unavailable to most adult defendants, for whom individual age, intelligence and experience is usually not taken into account. An exception arises when the child engages in an activity that is usually limited to adults. In this situation, the child is held to the reasonable person standard, with personal characteristics omitted from analysis.

61.   The emergency standard of care gives actors an extra measure of leniency when their behavior is assessed in a negligence claim. They are held to the standard of a reasonable person under the same emergency. This standard is not applied when the actor's own wrongful conduct caused the emergency to occur. Yarble should be liable.

62.   **Answer (B) is correct.** Jurisdictions using a "directness" or "intervening cause" approach to proximate cause tend to analyze the problem in terms of an interrupted or uninterrupted chain of events. An interruption would cut off the original wrongdoer's responsibility. Reasonably foreseeable events (including mishaps) that cause further harm to the victim generally are not treated as beyond the scope of the original wrongdoer's responsibility. In fact, one typical case of this kind is the doctor who negligently treats the injured person.

      Answer (A) is incorrect for the reason just given.

      Answer (C) is incorrect because courts employing a "scope of risk" or "scope of duty" analysis tend to treat reasonably foreseeable events (including mishaps) as within the scope of the original wrongdoer's responsibility. Some courts using this approach also speak of liability for events that occur before the "dust has settled" from the original event. Here, Adam was still in a precarious position when the doctor negligently treated him; thus, the dust had not settled.

      Answer (D) is incorrect because lack of control over the doctor's conduct is not relevant to the scope of liability question in this situation.

63.   **Answer (C) is correct.** A party whose conduct is careless may be held responsible even when a force of nature contributes to the occurrence of the accident. Here, in fact, one of the reasons Robbie's conduct is unreasonable is that it created an opportunity for a force of nature (the wind) to blow newspapers off the truck, which in turn created a foreseeable risk of harm to others using the roadway.

      Answer (A) is incorrect because, even in a jurisdiction that adheres to a "directness" or "intervening cause" test of proximate cause, a party whose negligence consists in creating an opportunity for a force of nature to cause harm will be liable for the harm when the force of nature acts.

      Answer (B) is incorrect because it assumes that once Fran establishes a cause in fact relationship between Robbie's conduct and her harm, she is entitled to recover. This is insufficient. Issues of scope of liability (proximate cause) still must be addressed.

      Answer (D) is incorrect because, under a "scope of risk" theory, reasonably foreseeable consequences of careless conduct are considered within the actor's responsibility. In this situation, contrary to the suggestion of answer (D), the jury is very likely to find that the risk of being struck by a stack of papers blown from the truck is reasonably foreseeable.

64.   Alternative liability deviates from principles of causation in tort law in two major respects. First, normally the plaintiff has the burden of proof to show causation. Under alternative liability, a defendant will have the burden of proof to show that its conduct did NOT cause harm to the plaintiff. Second, alternative liability accepts in principle the possibility that an "innocent" defendant — that is, a defendant that did not cause harm to the plaintiff — will bear the costs of compensation. Normally the risks and detriments of uncertainty or failure of proof fall on the plaintiff.

65.   **Answer (A) is correct.** Hardy must establish that it is more likely than not that had he been able to reach a 911 operator, Hannah would have survived, at least for a meaningfully longer time. Proving a negative is, of course, difficult, but that is a problem faced by plaintiffs in many tort cases.

       Answer (B) is incorrect because the burden of proof on causation lies with the plaintiff, not the defendant. This is true of the other elements of the prima facie case for negligence as well.

       Answer (C) is incorrect because foreseeability is not part of the determination of cause in fact. Foreseeability factors into the scope of liability (proximate cause) question, but not cause in fact.

       Answer (D) is incorrect because a failure to act can have a causal connection to harm. For example, a driver who fails to hit the brakes before hitting a pedestrian is a cause in fact of the pedestrian's injury. Moreover, Phone Co. (like the driver), has engaged in some action: it has operated the 911 emergency system. The problem is that it did not do a good enough job of making the system available to callers when the phone lines were very crowded. Even if this is viewed as a case of nonfeasance, however, Phone Co.'s failure to provide Hardy with a connection to 911 will be viewed as a cause in fact if, but for that failure, Hannah's life would have been extended meaningfully or saved.

66.   **Answer (D) is correct.** Directness-type approaches to proximate cause look for unbroken chains of events. Sometimes, they refer to consequences that "directly" flow from the negligent act. Criminal actors whose conduct intervenes between the originally negligent actor and the harm do not necessarily cut the chain of events. In fact, if the criminal actor merely does the harmful act, the risk of which was created by the defendant's negligence, most courts hold that the chain remains unbroken. This is not a certain result in a case such as the one here, where the criminal actor committed murder. But it is a reasonable argument that Paladin is liable.

       Answer (A) is incorrect because it assumes a categorical rule that a criminal actor cuts off the originally negligent party's responsibility. That is not true, as discussed above.

       Answer (B) is incorrect because lack of "control" does not vitiate liability. If a party creates the environment for a harm to occur, the party can be held liable even if the harm is caused immediately by an actor independent of the original wrongdoer. Moreover, it is arguable that Paladin had reason to know its instructions might be followed by a person who would read "Hit Man"; some such people are unsavory characters.

Answer (C) is incorrect because, viewed in context, it is not unreasonable to imagine that a person might follow the directions in the book and commit a murder.

67.   **Answer (B) is correct.** The facts strongly suggest that, but for Dan's repeated striking of Paula's car, Paula would not have been seen leaving the scene of an accident, reported to the police, and charged with hit-and-run driving. And of course, Paula would not have suffered emotional distress.

Answer (A) is incorrect because foreseeability is relevant to the cause in fact question.

Answer (C) is incorrect because, while it is often difficult to prove a negative — to prove what would have happened if not for defendant's conduct — there is no such problem here. The entire situation that left Paula an emotional wreck was brought about by Dan's initial act of striking Paula's car over and over.

Answer (D) is incorrect because more than one thing can be a cause in fact of harm. Here, it's possible that other factors contributed to Paula's suffering emotional distress. But as long as Dan's conduct was one factor, it qualifies.

68.   No, it does not. The but-for test requires that the occurrence be "necessary" in order for the harm to take place. If it is merely "sufficient," then the occurrence is usually held not to have been a but-for cause of the harm. For example, suppose that X shoots Q in the heart. X intends to kill Q, but unknown to X, Q has died a half hour beforehand, of a stroke. X's conduct — "sufficient" but not "necessary" to kill — is not a but-for cause of Q's death. Of course, the but-for test is not always used. The "substantial factor" test is more inclusive.

69.   **Answer (B) is correct.** The traditional view of causation holds that a negligent party is only responsible if the jury concludes that it is more likely than not that the party caused the harm suffered by the plaintiff. In this case, Paul had only 40% chance of survival even if diagnosed and treated properly. Thus, under the traditional rule, it cannot be said that "but for" Doc's negligent diagnosis, it is more likely than not that Paul would have survived.

Answer (A) is incorrect for the reasons just given.

Answer (C) is incorrect because under the "lost chance of survival" theory, courts permit recovery of a proportional amount of the plaintiff's damages when the defendant's negligence deprived the plaintiff of a significant chance of recovery. A 40% chance of recovery is probably significant. Thus, in this case, a court might allow plaintiff to recover 40% of the total loss. (Note that there are many different "lost chance" formulations. Most allow reduced damages, but they use different kinds of calculations.)

Answer (D) is incorrect because, as stated above, most courts adopting a "lost chance" theory award reduced damages.

70.   **Answer (C) is correct.** Dolores has the burden of persuasion on all elements of his claim, including cause in fact. Here, Dolores must show that she would have been able to escape had Carl not blocked the driveway. If this is not true, Carl's conduct would not be a but-for cause of the burglars' attack.

     Answer (A) is incorrect because it does not matter if a party's action plays only a minor role in bringing about the harm. As long as it was a but-for cause, the element is satisfied. Issues related to the degree of causation can be part of the proximate cause analysis.

     Answer (B) is incorrect because reasonable foreseeability of an injury is an issue related to scope of duty or proximate cause, not cause in fact.

     Answer (D) is incorrect because it suggests that Carl has the burden of persuasion on causation. As noted above, this is not the case.

71.   **Answer (B) is correct.** "Directness" approaches to proximate cause tend to look for unbroken chains of events. Many factors can affect whether the chain will be deemed broken. Among them are the passage of time between the negligent act and the harm, whether the harm occurs in a place quite different from where defendant's negligent act occurred, whether the type of harm was reasonably foreseeable, and the nature of any intervening acts. If the harm is most immediately brought about by an unforeseeable criminal actor, the chain is likely to be deemed broken. That was the case here. It was not reasonably foreseeable to one in Carl's position that leaving his car blocking Dolores's driveway would contribute to her being attacked by burglars.

     Answer (A) is incorrect because the language of that answer tracks "scope of duty" analyses, not "directness" analyses.

     Answer (C) is incorrect because the mere fact that a party's act is the first link in a chain of events leading to injury does not mean it is the direct cause of the injury.

     Answer (D) is incorrect because it is not enough that some harm was foreseeable from blocking the driveway. The harm that occurs must still be deemed the "direct" cause of the defendant's negligent act.

72.   **Answer (A) is correct.** This answer tracks the kind of terminology and approach a court using risk analysis would use. Generally speaking, a harm will be viewed as within the scope of risk brought about by an actor's careless conduct if the victim was among those to whom harm was reasonably foreseeable, and if the type of harm that occurred was a type that was reasonably foreseeable. Here, it is not likely that a reasonable person would think that blocking Dolores's driveway would create a risk of personal injury to her.

Answer (B) is incorrect because, as explained in connection with the previous question, this is the kind of analysis a court using a "directness" approach would bring to bear on the proximate cause issue.

Answers (C) and (D) are incorrect because they do not use risk analysis. (In addition, as discussed in connection with the previous question, they are faulty statements of "directness" analysis as well.)

73.   The strongest case for non-liability of the initially negligent defendant would involve unforeseeable criminal misconduct by another person. Imagine a parking garage that has been open for years in perfect safety, with no crimes or even accidents taking place on the scene. At the same time, it expressly disclaims taking safety precautions. The defendant owns the garage. Its negligence consists of not inspecting the swipe-key lock that long-term customers use to gain access to their vehicles. Unknown to the defendant, the lock sensor weakens in a way that any credit card will work to open the door. All other conditions in the garage are extremely safe. An intruder enters with a credit card and, acting on a fetish, kisses the feet of a customer against his will (a battery). (More serious harms might impel a court to rule against the garage in order to compensate the plaintiff.) If the intruder is captured and has enough assets to satisfy a judgment, that fact would make the case for non-liability of the garage even stronger.

74.   **Answer (D) is correct.** Many jurisdictions hold that people engaged in sporting activities assume the risks naturally associated with those activities. This is a "primary" form of assumption of risk that eliminates the duty of another participant to exercise reasonable care to avoid creating such risks. As a result, the injured party is not permitted to recover. It is very unlikely, however, that a court would hold that being struck by a cyclist is an inherent risk of jogging. Perhaps tripping on uneven pavement is an inherent risk, and maybe even colliding with another jogger, but the cyclist isn't even a participant in the sport; she was engaged in a different activity. If primary assumption of risk does not apply, then some jurisdictions still permit a defendant to assert an affirmative defense of secondary assumption of risk. That form of the defense generally requires a showing that the plaintiff voluntarily confronted the specific hazard to which he was exposed. That was not true here because the facts state that Earl did not know Fran was approaching. Thus, Earl did not assume the risk in the secondary sense, either.

      Answer (A) is incorrect because being hit by a cyclist is not an inherent risk of jogging.

      Answer (B) is incorrect for the same reason, and also because it is not at all clear that Fran's conduct was willful or reckless (which in some jurisdictions would overcome the primary assumption of risk claim). At best this is a jury question, and this might even be a situation in which the judge can decide as a matter of law that the party (here, Fran) did not act willfully or recklessly.

      Answer (C) is incorrect because, if primary assumption of risk applies, it defeats recovery entirely; it does not reduce recovery.

75.   **Answer (C) is correct.** The defendant need not have been aware of the plaintiff's assumption of risk at the time of the injury, and the plaintiff need not have communicated this assumption of risk to the defendant.

      Answer (A) is incorrect. Volition, or voluntariness, is an element of assumption of risk.

      Answer (B) is incorrect because most jurisdictions have merged implied assumption of risk together with comparative negligence. Both doctrines reduce, but do not eliminate, the plaintiff's recovery.

      Answer (D) is incorrect. Knowledge of the risk is an element of assumption of risk.

76.   **Answer (A) is correct.** The jury will be instructed that a person with special skill or experience is to be measured against a reasonable person with the same special skill or experi-

ence when determining the reasonableness of her conduct. If a reasonable person with Herrle's training would not have intervened, Herrle's recovery should be reduced.

Answer (B) is incorrect for the reason just given.

Answer (C) is incorrect because it assumes what the jury must decide: whether it was in fact unreasonable for Herrle to intervene. We cannot say as a matter of law that she acted unreasonably.

Answer (D) is incorrect because it begs the question at issue: whether Herrle acted reasonably under the circumstances. True, she would not have been harmed had she not intervened. But this does not resolve the question whether her recovery should be reduced.

NOTE: In this problem, it is also possible that Herrle will face a claim that the hazard she confronted was such an integral part of her job to care for Alzheimer's patients that she cannot prevail in a negligence action against one of the patients. The best way to see this as a doctrinal matter is as a question of limited duty: Because of her mental condition, Marshall did not owe a duty of reasonable care toward those whose job was, at least in part, to keep her safe from herself. If this is true, Herrle's action might fail completely.

77.   **Answer (C) is correct.** Even though Lina was an invitee to whom a duty of reasonable care was owed, Lina was also obligated to exercise reasonable care for her own safety. If the jury concludes that it was unreasonable under the circumstances for Lina to attempt to remove a jar in the way she did, and if her act was a substantial factor in her injury, the jury may reduce her award.

Answer (A) is incorrect because it fails to take account of the doctrine of comparative fault.

Answer (B) is incorrect because comparative fault requires a finding that the plaintiff failed to exercise ordinary care for her own safety. Even if Lina realized that it was risky to remove a jar from the stack, she will not be comparatively negligent if her conduct in doing so was not unreasonable.

Answer (D) is incorrect because, under a pure comparative fault system, the plaintiff may recover something even if her own negligence exceeded that of defendant. Thus, even if the jury concludes that Lina was 90% responsible, she can recover 10% of her losses.

78.   **Answer (D) is correct.** Some jurisdictions have abolished "secondary" assumption of risk. In those where the defense still exists, it is an affirmative defense that requires defendant to prove two facts: (1) that plaintiff recognized and appreciated the specific risk she was confronting; and (2) that plaintiff chose voluntarily to confront the risk. Under a system of comparative fault, the defense will reduce plaintiff's recovery. Here, if the jury finds that Lina knew and appreciated the risk that the stack of jars would fall, and chose voluntarily to confront it, it may reduce her award.

Answer (A) is incorrect because it speaks to the doctrine of "primary" assumption of risk, not secondary assumption of risk.

Answer (B) is incorrect because it inappropriately mixes the two forms of assumption of risk. The concept of a risk that is "inherent in the activity" it not typically viewed as a feature of secondary assumption of risk.

Answer (C) is incorrect because, as explained above, secondary assumption of risk reduces recovery according to principles of comparative fault. It is not a complete defense.

79.   As a general rule, a defendant's compliance with a statute is not a defense to negligence. In this respect tort law is asymmetrical; violation of a statute can often demonstrate duty and breach (under "negligence per se"), but compliance with a statute is usually not a defense or an excuse. Most courts will, however, permit a defendant to introduce compliance with a statute as relevant to its claim that it was not negligent. Also, occasionally a statute will provide that compliance is a complete defense to private negligence claims. Statutes that preempt common law tort claims establish yet another exception: When the defendant has complied with the statute, it is immune from a common law negligence claim.

80.   **Answer (D) is correct.** The contract is probably an adhesion contract because it was drafted by one party and appears to have been placed before the other party on a take-it-or-leave-it basis. This does not mean its exculpatory clause was unenforceable, however. Such clauses are enforceable unless they violate some important public policy. For example, courts have voided exculpatory clauses purporting to absolve operators of hospital emergency rooms of liability for negligence toward patients. Emergency rooms provide essential services that any member of the public may need at any moment, and the circumstances in which one goes to the emergency room seldom leave her with many alternatives. But courts have usually enforced exculpatory agreements that pertain to purely voluntary activities, particularly sporting activities. If Paul did not like this clause, he could have gone elsewhere. And if all other stables used similar agreements, he could have decided whether to sign or to forgo horseback riding.

Answer (A) is incorrect for the reasons just given.

Answer (B) is incorrect because an exculpatory clause need not be extremely specific in order to be enforceable. The language of this clause sufficiently put Paul on notice of Ed's limited liability.

Answer (C) is incorrect because the agreement, if otherwise enforceable, can be applied to both experienced and inexperienced riders. Put differently, there is no strong public policy forbidding stables from exculpating themselves from liability even to inexperienced riders. In fact, it is primarily from the claims of injured novices that stables will want to protect themselves most.

81. **Answer (C) is correct.** Courts hold that people who attend sporting events accept the risks inherent in that activity. This is a defense that completely defeats the claim because it amounts to a finding that the defendant did not owe the plaintiff a duty with regard to that injury. Thus, if Clifford had been hit by a flying hockey puck, he would not be able to recover. But that is not what happened. Clifford was injured by a risk that is not inherent in the game: flying glass from an improperly maintained barrier. A spectator does not "assume" that risk because fans have reason to expect that these barriers will protect them. Clifford's recovery should not be affected.

     Answer (A) is incorrect because, as explained above, this risk is not inherent in sitting so close to the ice at a hockey game. Also, the facts do not suggest that Sidney's failure to repair the barrier was reckless. It appears Sidney was merely negligent.

     Answer (B) is incorrect because, if being hit by glass fragments was not an inherent risk of attending a hockey game, there is no basis for reducing Clifford's recovery to any degree.

     Answer (D) is incorrect because merely choosing to attend the game does not amount to any form of assumption of risk. If the roof had caved in during the game, surely Clifford would have been able to recover.

82. First, contributory negligence is still the rule in a handful of jurisdictions. Second, most jurisdictions that have adopted comparative negligence limit its effect through the "not as great" or "not greater than" approach (both are sometimes called "modified" approaches), in effect holding plaintiffs to a more stringent standard of care. Like the original rule of contributory negligence, these versions of comparative negligence provide that a defendant whose share of fault was a significant factor in the plaintiff's injury (perhaps the defendant was 30% responsible, or even 50%) will completely escape liability because of the plaintiff was at fault.

83. Primary implied assumption of risk arises where the defendant did not breach a duty to the plaintiff; secondary implied assumption of risk arises where the defendant has breached a duty to the plaintiff and then, upon being sued by the plaintiff, raises "assumption of risk" as an affirmative defense. Often "secondary implied assumption of risk" claims strongly resemble claims of "contributory negligence." Before the onset of comparative negligence, courts were casual about distinguishing the two. The modern trend views implied secondary assumption of risk as equivalent to comparative negligence, and so the task of distinguishing them has returned to being relatively unimportant, although not for the same reason.

84. The mentally deficient plaintiff has hurt only herself; the mentally deficient defendant has hurt others. Because self-preservation is a powerful force, the courts can take a more relaxed stance about negligence that harms only the negligent party. This "inconsistency" also softens the harsh effects of contributory negligence.

85.   **Answer (D) is correct.** Blasting is categorized as an "abnormally dangerous activity" for which courts impose strict liability. Thus, Peter will not have to prove any negligence in order to hold BlastCo liable for the damage. Though the employer of an independent contractor is generally not liable for the torts of the independent contractor, there is an exception for certain "non-delegable duties." Generally speaking, activities that involve significant danger (usually called "inherently dangerous activities") are non-delegable because a person engaged in such conduct should not be able to avoid responsibility for its consequences by "delegating" the task to another person. If an inherently dangerous activity is non-delegable, then an abnormally dangerous activity certainly is also non-delegable.

      Answers (A), (B), and (C) are incorrect because Owner will be liable for harm caused by BlastCo's abnormally dangerous activity even if BlastCo was neither negligent nor reckless.

86.   **Answer (A) is correct.** Blasting is an abnormally dangerous activity because, among other reasons, damage from the blast itself cannot be prevented in all cases even with the exercise of ordinary care. But this is not true of hauling. Normally, if one exercises reasonable care, damage from hauling can be prevented. In addition, few if any of the other factors mentioned in *Restatement (Second) of Torts* § 520 (which define an abnormally dangerous activity) are satisfied. (Among the reasons: Heavy trucks are common in most places. Though harm can be great when such a truck overturns or otherwise is involved in a mishap, the likelihood of a mishap is probably no greater than with other vehicles.) Thus, Owner will only be liable if Paul can prove that it was negligent in driving over that road with such a heavy truck.

      Answer (B) is incorrect because what makes blasting abnormally dangerous is the use of dynamite, not other activities (such as hauling debris) associated with it.

      Answer (C) is incorrect because, as discussed above, hauling debris is not an abnormally dangerous activity.

      Answer (D) is incorrect because a party can be negligent, and liable, for driving a very heavy vehicle over a street even if there is no specific prohibition. It might be difficult for Paul to prove it was negligent to do so, in the absence of a specific prohibition, but he might be able to muster the evidence.

87.   **Answer (B) is correct.** Though at one point some courts did not apply the strict liability rule to concussion damage caused by blasting, all courts now do. Thus, Owner will be strictly liable to Porter.

Answer (A) is incorrect because, as discussed above, Owner is strictly liable.

Answer (C) is incorrect because it is irrelevant that there was no trespass by a physical object such as a rock. The shockwave caused by the blast brought about the damage.

Answer (D) is incorrect because keeping a rickety old barn does not constitute assumption of risk that it will be blown down by a dynamite blast.

88. **Answer (C) is correct.** Storing huge quantities of gasoline might be an abnormally dangerous activity, but liability will only extend to harm caused by the characteristic of that activity that makes it abnormally dangerous. Presumably, that characteristic is the explosiveness of gasoline vapor. Had Patty's car been destroyed by an explosion of the tank, Patty could hold OilCo strictly liable. But in this case, the damage was not caused by the explosive quality of gasoline. It was caused by a combination of the weight of the full tank and the defective steel in the platform. A collapse of this kind would have occurred with any heavy substance in the tank, including water. Weight alone does not make the activity abnormally dangerous, nor does the use of steel. Thus, unless facts appear that are not given in this question, it is not abnormally dangerous to store gasoline in a tank on top of a platform. Patty can only hold OilCo liable if OilCo was negligent.

Answer (A) is incorrect for the reasons just given.

Answer (B) is incorrect because violation of an industry custom is not negligence in itself. It is only some evidence of negligence.

Answer (D) is incorrect because OilCo need not have built the platform to be liable for damage it caused. It can be held liable if it negligently maintained the platform or failed to conduct reasonable inspections.

89. Although driving a truck along a highway is not an abnormally dangerous activity, driving a tanker truck filled with gasoline poses a risk of extremely great harm in the event of a mishap that causes the gasoline to spill and ignite. Reasonable care, whether in the manner of driving or in the maintenance of the truck and trailer, will not eliminate the risk of this great harm. Although tanker trucks are common on the highways, their use is not common among the general public (only special companies use them). For at least these reasons, the activity can be classified as abnormally dangerous, and GasCo should be strictly liable to Popper.

90. **Answer (A) is correct.** Two of the six factors mentioned in *Restatement (Second) of Torts* § 520 for determining whether an activity qualifies as "abnormally dangerous" are the probability that harm will occur (the higher the probability, the more likely the activity qualifies as abnormally dangerous) and the likely degree of harm it causes (the greater the likely harm, the greater the likelihood the activity is abnormally dangerous). The *Restatement*

test is not categorical — that is, there is no precise formula for when an activity qualifies. But the more factors are satisfied, the more likely the activity meets the test.

Answer (B) is incorrect because the *Restatement* formulation suggests that if the danger from the activity can be prevented by the exercise of reasonable care, it is *less* likely to qualify as abnormally dangerous. The case would be resolved according to negligence principles instead.

Answer (C) is incorrect because the more common the activity in the community, the *less* likely it will be classified as abnormally dangerous.

Answer (D) is incorrect because a physical intrusion is not required for this tort.

91.   **Answer (B) is correct.** Conducting experiments with chemicals that can explode and release toxic chemicals to neighboring property is the kind of activity that historically qualifies for the strict liability "abnormally dangerous activities" claim. From the facts, we cannot tell how likely it was that the activity would lead to harm, nor the amount of harm that would likely occur if there was a mishap. But chemical experimentation can often be very dangerous. In addition, this was done in the basement of a house, probably in a residential neighborhood, which might not be common or appropriate for this location. Though unclear, the fact that the explosion was unexpected and inexplicable suggests that even the exercise of reasonable care would not prevent it from occurring. The potential social benefit from the activity might be relatively great, but whether that is true for an amateur scientist engaged in research that hasn't been particularly fruitful for professional scientists is somewhat doubtful. If the activity fits into that category, it will not be necessary to prove negligence, making it a preferred claim for Curly to assert.

      Answer (A) is incorrect because this is a case of injury to the person of the plaintiff, not interference with plaintiff's use and enjoyment of property. Thus, this is not the type of harm that the law of private nuisance is designed to redress.

      Answer (C) is incorrect because the facts suggest that negligence will be difficult to prove. Ari was being "careful[]," and the explosion was "inexplicabl[e]" and "unexpected[]," making it less likely that he was negligent.

      Answer (D) is incorrect because trespass requires an *intentional* entry onto the land of another without permission. Here, the entry of the chemicals was not intentional. Ari neither wished this to happen nor knew it was substantially certain to happen. Thus, trespass is not a viable claim.

92.   **Answer (A) is correct.** Under *Restatement (Second) of Torts* § 520, the easier it is to eliminate the risk of harm through the exercise of reasonable care, the less likely the court will classify the activity as abnormally dangerous. If Ahmid can lessen the noise and avoid

spreading the dust simply by enclosing his work area, his activity is less likely to be classified as abnormally dangerous.

Answer (B) is incorrect because the plaintiff's ability to avoid the harmful effects of the defendant's conduct by limiting her use of her own land should not matter to an action for carrying on an abnormally dangerous activity. Rosa should not be forced to choose between using her back porch and becoming ill, on the one hand, and not using her back porch and staying healthy, on the other.

Answer (C) is incorrect because the plaintiff's ability to avoid the harm by spending money should not affect her recovery for harm caused by defendant's abnormally dangerous activity. While we must all accept certain dangers associated with everyday life, if the factors relevant to characterizing Ahmid's activity as abnormally dangerous suggest that the activity qualifies, it is not fair to force Rosa to limit the use of her own property to avoid the harm.

Answer (D) is incorrect because an activity is even more likely to be deemed abnormally dangerous if it affects a larger number of people. Thus, this factor probably increases, rather than reduces, Rosa's chances of success in her suit against Ahmid.

93.   **Answer (D) is correct.** If the defendant's activity affects use and enjoyment of land by a large number of people in roughly same way, it is less likely to be classified as a private nuisance, and more likely to be classified as a public nuisance that should be redressed in an action by the local prosecutor. Here, dust from Ahmid's work would "fill the air for miles around." This suggests that the problem is more of a public nuisance, and reduces Rosa's chances of prevailing in her private nuisance action.

Answer (A) is incorrect because the defendant's ability to eliminate the harm increases, rather than decreases, the plaintiff's chances of prevailing. This is because a private nuisance action may be based on negligent conduct (as well as on intentional conduct and on conduct that would subject the actor to strict liability for carrying on an abnormally dangerous activity). Here, to use the Learned Hand formula, if the cost to Ahmid of enclosing his work area is less than the harm he is causing by spreading dust for miles around, not enclosing the area is negligence. Rosa's chances of prevailing are improved, not hurt, by this fact.

Answer (B) is incorrect because Ahmid's activity is the very reason Rosa has to go inside. In other words, not being able to use the back porch without suffering from the effects of noise and dust is exactly what makes Ahmid's activity a nuisance: it affects Rosa's use and enjoyment of her property.

Answer (C) is incorrect because of the "thin skull" rule. As long as a normally constituted person would suffer substantial interference with the use and enjoyment of land, the fact that Rosa is more sensitive than most will not affect her recovery. Behavior that would be tortious toward an average person does not lose its tortious character when it affects a sensitive person in a greater way.

94. **Answer (D) is correct.** The facts state that the lift snapped "[d]ue to factors of which CE had not reason to be aware." If that is true, this appears to have been an accident without fault. Even though harm occurred, CE is not liable for negligence in the handling of the drum. (Perhaps Diane could make a different kind of claim, such as a claim that CE should not have been using a forklift to move the drum. But that is not the claim stated in the problem.)

    Answer (A) is incorrect because, as explained above, the evidence strongly suggests that CE exercised reasonable care in its handling of the drum.

    Answer (B) is incorrect because CE's experience with handling chemicals did not impose on it a "higher duty." The jury would be entitled to consider CE's experience in deciding whether CE in fact breached its duty, but the duty is the same as it would be even if CE did not have the experience: reasonable care under the circumstances. CE appears to have exercised reasonable care, even taking account of CE's experience.

    Answer (C) is incorrect because using procedures that meet or exceed industry standards is not a per se test for reasonableness. It is some evidence of reasonable care, but not conclusive proof.

95. **Answer (D) is correct.** Nuisance is the substantial and unreasonable interference with plaintiff's use and enjoyment of property. It can be based on conduct that qualifies as intentional, negligent, or abnormally dangerous. Here, Peg Co.'s conduct interferes with Al's sleep to a degree that a jury might find substantial. In addition, a jury might find it unreasonable impose this burden on Al. (This would be especially true if a reasonable company would make the alarms to be less sensitive or silence them more quickly.)

    Public nuisances are those that affect the entire community in much the same way.

    Answer (A) is incorrect because the noise from Peg Co. vehicles affects Al differently than it affects other people. Of course, others might suffer in the same way as Al, but only those whose homes are as close to the garage as Al's. This is more a private matter than a community-wide matter.

    Answer (B) is incorrect for two reasons. First, Peg Co.'s behavior is intentional. "Intent" may be shown either by a desire to bring about the event or by knowledge that the event is substantially certain to occur. Though Peg Co. probably does not want the alarms to go off when there is no criminal activity, it certainly is aware that this is happening. Second, an action for nuisance may be based on intentional conduct, but does not have to be based on such conduct.

Answer (C) is incorrect because there is no suggestion in the facts that creation of the noise is an abnormally dangerous activity. In fact, it would not qualify as such because most of the factors listed in *Restatement (Second) of Torts* § 520 are not satisfied. (For example, the risk of harm is not very great. The harm itself, while not negligible, is not as great as harm that normally qualifies as abnormally dangerous; car alarms are commonly used; and the risk can be eliminated or substantially reduced by the exercise of reasonable care.)

96.   **Answer (D) is correct.** Justice Blackburn set forth a standard that held a party strictly liable for keeping something on one's property that can do harm if it escapes. This is what happened here. The instruction states the essence of Blackburn's standard: if MotorCo's testing posed a substantial risk of harm to those outside its property as a result of the escape of one of its cars, MotorCo is strictly liable for the harm caused.

Answer (A) is incorrect because this is not a case that fits into Blackburn's exception for "traffic on the highways." MotorCo was not engaging in normal highway traffic, and Potter did not voluntarily take to the road with MotorCo's experimental car.

Answer (B) is incorrect because Justice Blackburn did not frame his standard in terms of the "non-natural" use of land. (It was Cairns in the House of Lords who stated that standard.)

Answer (C) is incorrect because Justice Blackburn rejected this standard. As stated above, he viewed this as a case in which strict liability could be imposed.

97.   **Answer (C) is correct.** Recovery on an "abnormally dangerous activity" theory requires proof that the type of harm suffered was caused by a feature of the activity that made it abnormally dangerous. Here, that feature was the explosiveness of the fuel (greater than the explosiveness of regular automobile fuels). Because the harm was caused by a collision with Potter's car, and not by an explosion, MotorCo is not strictly liable.

Answer (A) is incorrect because it fails to account for the requirement that the harm be caused by the "abnormally dangerous" feature of the activity.

Answer (B) is incorrect because it assumes that if the balance of social benefit against risk favors the benefit, MotorCo may not be held liable. This is not correct. The six-part standard set forth in *Restatements (Second) of Torts* § 520 is not a categorical test; an activity need not meet each element. The court is to view the activity as a whole in light of all the elements, and decide whether it qualifies. Thus, even an activity the benefit of which outweighs the risk it creates can qualify as abnormally dangerous.

Answer (D) is incorrect because it has the element backward. Under the *Restatement* test, if the harm can be prevented by the exercise of reasonable care, it is *less* likely that it will qualify as abnormally dangerous.

98. Statutes and case law often make exceptions for *trespass*, when the plaintiff has unlawfully entered the defendant's land, and for *provocation*, when the animal was minding its own business and plaintiff instigated an unnecessary encounter with the animal

99. The *Restatement (Second) of Torts* offers multifactor balancing rather than a bright-line rule. Balancing is more familiar to negligence than strict liability, which seeks categories. Factor (A), which looks for a high risk of harm, and factor (D), which asks whether the activity is uncommon, raise questions that are integral to assigning strict liability to an activity, yet they are not dispositive. Other factors could outweigh these two. Thus, an activity that is neither especially risky nor especially common — that is, an activity that seems to fit within the more ordinary category of negligence — could fall within the *Restatement (Second) of Torts'* test for strict liability.

100. An activity governed by strict liability — for example, blasting with dynamite — can cause a variety of injuries, but in order to fall within strict liability, the injuries must relate to the dangerous propensities of the activity. This requirement resembles the "risk rule" (or risk analysis) of proximate cause, which uses foreseeability to limit liability for harms caused by the defendant's negligence. For example, not every harm caused by blasting is actionable in strict liability. The classic case of Foster v. Preston Mill Co., 268 P.2d 645 (Wash. 1954), held that a defendant that engaged in blasting would not be liable for a particular result that appeared odd or unforeseeable to the court (minks killing their young), even though the court accepted that the defendant's blasting caused this result. For another example, consider the keeping of a wild animal. If the wild animal does something harmful that is related to its dangerous propensities (such as biting), the keeper is strictly liable, but if the wild animal does something harmful that is unrelated to its dangerous propensities, the keeper is not strictly liable.

101. **Answer (B) is correct**. Eric's most viable argument to defeat Kyle's claim is that Eric's conduct has created a nuisance to the general public, and not particularly to Eric. This is not a strong argument, however, because residents whose homes back up to this alley are likely to be affected far more by the trash heap than are other people. As we will see, the argument is at least more viable than the others set forth.

    Answer (A) is incorrect because the "live and let live" maxim does not apply to conduct that creates a substantial interference with use and enjoyment of property.

    Answer (C) is incorrect because it does not matter that the trash has not "invaded" Kyle's property; this is not a prerequisite for the tort of nuisance. In addition, the facts demonstrate that the trash has, indeed, "interfered" with Kyle's use and enjoyment of his land.

    Answer (D) is incorrect because Kyle's use and enjoyment has been affected even though his car was not scratched.

102. **Answer (C) is correct.** Nuisance requires a substantial interference with the plaintiff's use and enjoyment of property. Some courts hold that it also must be an unreasonable interference, partly in the sense that the benefits of the activity do not outweigh the gravity of the harm to the plaintiff. Darren's strongest defense is probably that seeing people in various states of undress is not a substantial interference with Samantha's use and enjoyment of her land, and that the benefit of operating a facility of this kind (in which people unavoidably engage in somewhat strange activity from time to time) outweighs the offense Samantha suffers.

Answer (A) is incorrect because it is not enough to say that the plaintiff can look away. She has a right to keep her eyes open while on her property. The real question is the degree of offense she suffers and the relative merit of First Step's activity as compared with the offense Samantha suffers.

Answer (B) is incorrect because a majority of courts hold that "coming to the nuisance" is not a per se defense to a nuisance action. The court may take into consideration that the defendant was there first when it decides the appropriate remedy (such as whether to enjoin the activity), but it does not affect the basic question of whether defendant is creating an actionable nuisance.

Answer (D) is incorrect because the public interest in allowing such facilities to operate, standing alone, does not provide a defense. As explained above, the court must weigh the value of the activity against the harm it causes ("unreasonable" interference), and must also consider the degree of harm suffered by the plaintiff ("substantial" interference).

103.   **Answer (C) is correct.** These facts give rise to a simple products liability case based on manufacturing defect. Courts hold that such cases may be brought on a strict liability theory,
which is extremely easy to prove if the defect is known. Because the facts indicate that the
handle was defective, this essentially leaves only the question of whether the defect was a
cause in fact of her harm, and that will be simple in this case. It does not matter that Diane
did not purchase the car.

   Answer (A) is incorrect because a negligence case is necessarily more difficult to prove,
even aided by the doctrine of res ipsa loquitur. To prevail, Diane will have to demonstrate
that this is the type of defect that usually results from negligence in the manufacturing
process, something she does not need to show under the strict products liability theory.

   Answer (B) is incorrect because the facts do not indicate that there was an express warranty
covering this kind of situation.

   Answer (D) is incorrect for the reasons given above.

104.   The implied warranty of fitness for a particular purpose arises between a buyer and seller
when the buyer communicates to the seller a particular need, and the seller understands that
the buyer is relying on the seller's expertise and advice. For purposes of products liability,
a product without flaws can become the basis of liability when the seller gives advice to the
buyer about a product, the buyer purchases the product and uses it as the seller advises, and
the buyer suffers injury.

105.   **Answer (D) is correct.** Pamela's case is based on an alleged design defect. It is not a typical design defect case, in which some basic feature of the car causes an accident, but the cell
phone is part of the car nevertheless, and if it is unreasonably dangerous to equip a car with
that appliance, the car can be viewed as defective. Today, courts favor a "risk-utility" test for
determining design defect. Thus, if the risks created by having a cell phone in the car outweigh its benefits, the car can be deemed defective.

   Answer (A) is incorrect because plaintiff in a products liability case need not have been
exposed involuntarily to the defective product in order to recover. Indeed, in most products
cases, it is the user of the product who sues.

   Answer (B) is incorrect because most courts do not require that the dangers have been
known at the time of manufacture. It is sufficient if the dangers would have been discovered by a reasonably prudent manufacturer conducting a reasonable level of testing.

Answer (C) is incorrect because a plaintiff in a products liability suit need not prove that the seller or manufacturer made any misrepresentations. Though a products case can be based on a misrepresentation, it is not a required element of proof.

106. **Answer (C) is correct.** Courts permit injured bystanders and others who were not using the product to bring products liability suits.

Answer (A) is incorrect for the reason just given.

Answer (B) is incorrect because reliance is not an element of a products liability action.

Answer (D) is incorrect because a products liability plaintiff may recover both for personal injuries and property damage.

107. Requiring that a plaintiff prove a reasonable alternative design increases her costs of litigating. She has to find expert evidence in order to reach a jury. Fewer valid claims might reach the courts when this standard is used. Critics also fault the requirement for importing negligence reasoning into strict products liability, thereby harming the general "enterprise liability" project of making manufacturers internalize the costs of product-caused injury. The requirement is also at odds with "generic products liability," which condemns entire categories of products, like cigarettes, as unreasonably dangerous. Many observers favor generic products liability. However, comment *e* to section 2(B) of the *Third Restatement* recognizes the possibility of a "manifestly unreasonable design," which might be extended to some generic products liability claims.

108. **Answer (D) is correct.** Assumption of risk (particularly assumption of risk that also constitutes comparative negligence) is a recognized defense to a products liability action. Putting a muffin in your mouth after noticing that there is something sharp embedded in it is probably both the voluntary confrontation of a known hazard and unreasonably dangerous. Homer's recovery is likely to be reduced as a result.

Answer (A) is incorrect because a plaintiff in a products liability case need not have been the purchaser of the product.

Answer (B) is incorrect because the seller of a product is a proper defendant in a product liability action.

Answer (C) is incorrect because, even if the nail was placed in the muffin by a person other than Maggie's, Maggie's sold the defective muffin. Strict liability applies.

109. **Answer (C) is correct.** If the nail got into the muffin after Bart's sold it to Maggie's, Bart's did not sell a defective muffin. Thus, Bart's will prevail in the products liability action.

Answer (A) is incorrect because, as noted already, a person need not be the purchaser to be a proper plaintiff in a products liability action.

Answer (B) is incorrect because Maggie's negligence is irrelevant to Homer's case against Bart's. Homer will win if the muffin left Bart's in a defective condition. Because it did not, Bart's is not liable.

Answer (D) is incorrect because any entity in the chain of distribution is a proper defendant if the product left that entity's hands in a defective condition. Here, of course, it did not.

110. **Answer (B) is correct.** Under the *Restatement (Third) of Torts: Products Liability*, the plaintiff's own fault may be used to reduce her recovery in a product liability action. A jury might view plaintiff's having tried to skate down a hill the first time she donned a pair of in-line skates as an act of comparative fault. This will reduce her recovery against RollersInc.

Answer (A) is incorrect because any negligence on the part of Joni's parents in buying the in-line skates does not affect the liability of RollersInc to Joni. Put differently, the negligence of Joni's parents, if any, will not be imputed to Joni so as to reduce her recovery.

Answer (C) is incorrect because a manufacturer is responsible not only for injuries to intended users, but also to others who might foreseeably use the product. This is an application of the "foreseeable misuse" doctrine, under which a manufacturer is liable for foreseeable misuses of its product.

Answer (D) is incorrect because the cost of the skates is irrelevant to whether they were defective.

111. **Answer (A) is correct.** As the source of the skates, RollersInc played a role in bringing about the harm Sally suffered. Cause in fact is an easy test to satisfy; a party responsible to any degree is a cause in fact.

Answer (B) is incorrect because RollersInc might be successful in arguing that Sally's modification of the skates so fundamentally changed their design, and was so unforeseeable (given the difficulty of accomplishing it), that RollersInc should not be viewed as a proximate cause of Sally's injury.

Answer (C) is incorrect because Sally might well have assumed the risk. She modified the skates for the purpose of achieving great speed. Her experience in skating for about an hour before her accident also probably added to her appreciation of the dangers posed by the skates as she had modified them. Thus, RollersInc has a viable argument that Sally voluntarily confronted a known and appreciated hazard.

Answer (D) is incorrect because Sally's modification might constitute an unforeseeable misuse of the skates. Though sellers are responsible for foreseeable misuses, they are not liable for unforeseeable ones. Because the wheel brackets were welded in place and were very difficult to modify, it is likely that a reasonable manufacturer in the position of RollersInc would not think it very likely that someone might make this modification. If this argument is accepted, RollersInc will defeat Sally's case.

112. **Answer (A) is correct.** This is a manufacturing defect case. Under the *Restatement (Third) of Torts: Products Liability*, and the law as it has developed in all jurisdictions, such cases may be brought on a strict liability theory. Section 2 of the *Restatement* provides that a product "contains a manufacturing defect when the product departs from its intended design even though all possible care was exercised in the preparation and marketing of the product." Thus, all Gordon will need to prove is that the skate left the hands of Skatz with a deviation from its design that caused him harm.

Answer (B) is incorrect because Skatz will be held strictly liable even if it would not be economically feasible for it to institute additional quality control procedures that would have caught this defect. This is the essence of strict liability in the present context.

Answer (C) is incorrect because it does not matter that Skatz exceeds what would be considered reasonable care in its quality control measures. It is strictly liable for a manufacturing defect.

Answer (D) is incorrect because the law permits an injured person to recover from any seller along the chain of production, including the original manufacturer. Of course, if a product has been altered before it reaches the plaintiff, entities earlier in the chain might not be liable for the alteration (though sometimes they are responsible), but that is not the case here in any event. The skate left Skatz's hands in a defective condition. Skatz is liable even though others, such as the store from which Gordon bought the skates, might also be liable.

113. **Answer (C) is correct.** Under the *Restatement (Third) of Torts: Products Liability*, comparative negligence is a partial defense. Here, Danny ran a red light, which appears to be negligent. The jury should reduce Danny's recovery.

Answer (A) is incorrect because recent authority, including the *Third Restatement*, rejects the consumer expectations test of defect. Instead, the courts use a risk-utility balance.

Answer (B) is incorrect because compliance with safety standards is relevant evidence of reasonable care, but hardly dispositive. A car that meets standards still may be found to have been designed defectively.

Answer (D) is incorrect because Danny did not assume the risk. There is no suggestion in the facts that he knew the door's protective beams were not as strong as those used in other cars.

114. **Answer (C) is correct.** A person who is injured by a defective product is a proper plaintiff even if she was not the purchaser (or even the user) of the product. The fact is irrelevant.

Answers (A), (B), and (D) are incorrect for the reason explained above.

115. The post-sale duty to warn dates back to the case of Comstock v. General Motors Corp., 99 N.W. 2d 627 (Mich. 1959). There the court held that an automobile manufacturer had to inform owners of this product after a latent design defect was discovered. Courts accepting this duty find that it is owed to users of the product. The manufacturer must act reasonably to find these users and communicate with them. The standard in evaluating this claim is negligence, not strict liability.

116. **Answer (B) is correct.** Severe emotional distress is not an element of the prima facie case for defamation.

    Answer (A) is incorrect because a false statement about a person's embezzlement tends to lower the reputation of that person, and harm to reputation is a central element of the prima facie case for defamation.

    Answer (C) is incorrect for the same reason.

    Answer (D) is incorrect because "publication," or the revelation of the defamatory communication to third parties, is an element of the prima facie case for defamation.

117. **Answer (A) is correct.** As a public official, Bumpkin must show that the Succotash Times acted either with a desire to lie or with reckless disregard for the truth of the statement it published. If its reporter should have been able to tell that Magoo was mentally incompetent, publishing Magoo's comments may satisfy the "actual malice" requirement of this tort.

    Answer (B) is incorrect because any "right to privacy" that Bumpkin asserts, or holds, does not affect his status as a defamation plaintiff.

    Answer (C) is incorrect, even though it may appear to show "actual malice." The requirement of "actual malice" is not fulfilled by proving animus, however. Rather, the defendant must have either intended to tell a lie or been reckless about the truth.

    Answer (D) is incorrect because media defendants do not become more liable, or less liable, when they choose to employ fact-checkers or print Corrections notices.

118. This situation arises where the defendant has a defamatory message and packages it with other words that make the statement formally or literally not false. For example, "I say she committed adultery with Rick Samson"; "Ask yourself whether he looted twenty thousand from his company"; "If I'm not mistaken, these books don't add up and she hid the money in her own private checking account;" "In my opinion, he is an unregistered child molester with a 1999 conviction for felony sexual assault"; and so forth. Speakers cannot escape liability by intoning a few 'magic words' to accompany the defamatory message.

119. **Answer (C) is correct.** This question addresses what courts used to call "innuendo" — the meaning of an ambiguous statement. Given what Gay is famous for and the subtext surrounding the reporters' question, a listener would infer that Gay was saying that McHew throws spitballs.

Answer (A) is incorrect because we don't know whether McHew has consented to anything.

Answer (B) is incorrect because the words are not innocuous and could harm McHew's reputation.

Answer (D) is incorrect because (among other reasons) we don't know whether Gay was offering an opinion on a matter of public comment.

120. Not entirely satisfactorily. The class of potentially defamatory statements is nearly infinite. Courts modify the *Restatement* formulation slightly to hold that a statement is *not* defamatory unless it is likely to cause a substantial number of people to avoid the plaintiff or hold her in less esteem. Although this approach does not resolve the definitional question, it does spare courts from having to hear eccentric claims of defamation.

121. **Answer (B) is correct.** Under the common law of defamation, the dead cannot be defamed.

      Answer (A) is incorrect because the defendant made no claims about Shipley Shipping.

      Answer (C) is incorrect because we have no information on the amount of time that has passed since publication.

      Answer (D) could be correct, but we do not have enough information to so conclude. It is possible that the behavior of Channel 7 news was sufficiently egregious to overcome the limited protections of the First Amendment.

122. **Answer (A) is correct.** Slander per se is a rule that eases the plaintiff's burden of proof. It rests on the premise that, as was stated, certain common accusations have predictable effects. Making each plaintiff prove individual harm would be costly.

      Answer (B) is incorrect even though it is generally accurate: This sentence does not offer an argument in favor of slander per se.

      Answer (C) is incorrect for similar reasons. This sentence offers an argument in favor of treating libel and slander differently, while the slander per se rule treats slander more like libel.

      Answer (D) is incorrect because slander per se applies to both business activity and the plaintiff's private life.

123. **Answer (C) is correct.** The First Amendment, like the rest of the Bill of Rights, presents limits to government power. The opportunity to criticize government officials is more fundamental to free speech than the opportunity to criticize the more eclectic, often apolitical, "public figures." Accordingly, public officials have more onerous obstacles when they sue for defamation.

Answer (A) is incorrect for the reasons just stated above.

Answer (B) is incorrect for the same reasons; in addition to being unsuccessful to support the point, this claim is probably not true.

Answer (D) is incorrect because even though public officials do enjoy relative immunity from defamation liability, the rationale for that relative immunity does not support making them suffer as plaintiffs.

124. **Answer (A) is correct** — a categorically accurate statement.

    Answer (B) is incorrect because justification (or lack thereof) is not part of defamation law.

    Answer (C) is incorrect because even actual malice is not sufficient to support a defamation claim, if the statement is true.

    Answer (D) is incorrect because invasions of privacy do not generate defamation liability.

125. **Answer (C) is correct.** Lawrie enjoys a broad privilege to speak freely (and even defamatorily) in the well of the legislature.

    Answer (A) is incorrect because a legislator's remarks need not relate reasonably to a legislative endeavor in order for the speaker to escape liability.

    Answer (B) is incorrect because Hilton may not be a public figure, and if he were, his defamation would be *harder* to prosecute, not easier.

    Answer (D) is the least incorrect of the three incorrect answers. Answer (C) is better than (D) because it identifies Lawrie's status as a legislator. Without reference to that status, Lawrie's safe harbor to engage in defamation becomes much more questionable. To the extent answer (D) implies some general privilege to defame in the context of debate on a matter of public interest, it is incorrect.

126. **Answer (A) is correct.** Defamation law reluctantly recognizes that litigation often has the effect of hurting a person's reputation, as a side consequence of the matter being litigated. It tries to mitigate this harm by requiring a reasonable relation to the issues raised in the proceeding.

    Answer (B) sounds good, perhaps, but says almost nothing. Defamation in a judicial proceeding often has nothing to do with "a matter of common public concern," to the extent that phrase refers to government.

    Answer (C) is incorrect, even though it is not far from the correct Answer (A). It exaggerates the speaker's duty, and suggests a negligence standard that is not in fact used.

    Answer (D) is incorrect: The privilege applies to civil cases.

127. Some citizens are so famous and powerful that they are all-purpose public figures, and the First Amendment protects a wide range of commentary about them. According to Gertz v. Robert Welch, Inc., 418 U.S. 323 (1974), such a person must enjoy either "pervasive power and influence" or "fame and notoriety." A larger number of potential plaintiffs are limited-purpose public figures, who may be discussed freely with respect to the issue or controversy for which they gained fame. Typically the defendant in such a defamation claim would have to show that the plaintiff sought this public role and participated voluntarily in a controversy.

128. **Answer (D) is correct.** An invasion of privacy claim of this kind — intrusion upon seclusion — turns on whether the plaintiff had a reasonable expectation of privacy.

    Answer (A) is incorrect because truth is a defense to defamation, not invasion of privacy.

    Answer (B) is incorrect because hotel guests have a legitimate expectation of privacy that covers this problem. Their rooms can be entered for cause, but not wiretapped for no good reason.

    Answer (C) is incorrect because whether disclosure is "repugnant" or not is not at issue in privacy claims.

129. **Answer (D) is correct.** To prosecute this version of the privacy tort — disclosure of private facts — a plaintiff must show "publicity" (*Restatement (Second) of Torts* § 652D, comment *a*), which means publication to the public at large or to a large group of people. Gossip within a limited circle does not satisfy this element.

    Answer (A) is incorrect because even if this "legitimate public concern" criterion is fulfilled, the "publicity" criterion remains fatal to the claim.

    Answer (B) is incorrect because the "highly offensive to a reasonable person" criterion is not used in the disclosure version of the privacy tort.

    Answer (C) is incorrect because the "public figure" criterion is not used in the disclosure version of the privacy tort.

130. Like various freedoms — of speech, mobility, and conscience among others — privacy is a cherished human right. If tort law were to be indifferent to privacy, most people would agree that it had failed to recognize something important. A legal concept of privacy also helps indirectly to check the power of other actors. Such a concern may underlie the Fourth Amendment condemnation of unreasonable searches and seizures — government would become a menace if it did not have to respect privacy. Privacy could be, and is, legislated as a public law, with tort law kept out of it. Statutes and the Constitution protect privacy. Adding a tort remedy strengthens these protections by empowering citizens to enforce their privacy rights.

131. **Answer (B) is correct.** By filing a claim, Mulcahy disclosed her own private facts. The Supreme Court has held in several cases that the media are not liable for invasion of privacy when they obtain information about individuals lawfully, through public records, and publish it.

Answer (A) is incorrect because Mulcahy's privacy claim is unlikely to prevail. (Her claim for intentional infliction of emotional distress is also unlikely to prevail.)

Answer (C) is incorrect because news disclosed need not be a matter of public significance in order for a media defendant to escape liability.

Answer (D) is incorrect because the publication of this information is not outrageous.

132. **Answer (B) is correct.** Privacy law is generally unconcerned with the distinction between true and false disclosures.

Answer (A) is incorrect because the privacy tort overlaps with other torts, and can be redundant.

Answer (C) is incorrect because individuals' interests in privacy is a major justification for the tort.

Answer (D) is incorrect because "newsworthiness" is salient to many privacy cases, especially those involving media defendants.

133. **Answer (C) is correct.** A corporation cannot bring a claim for invasion of privacy. Its rights to privacy are protected by trade secrets law and similar special categories.

Answer (A) is incorrect because deceit is not an element of invasion of privacy.

Answer (B) is incorrect because "privilege" has nothing to do with this problem. Tarpala made her way onto the factory floor with a ruse. Her deceit might relate to a trespass claim, but not a privacy claim.

Answer (D) is incorrect because the problem states that Tarpala's client used the information for competitive advantage against the plaintiff.

134. **Answer (A) is correct.** Packaging of consumer goods falls within the traditional heart of this tort, which has focused on using the plaintiff's likeness for purposes of advertising.

Answer (B) is incorrect because courts give magazines broad license to use photographs in their reporting of 'newsworthy' events.

Answer (C) is incorrect because giving a character in a work of fiction the name of a real person does not, without more, give rise to liability for invasion of privacy, even if the character is unattractive.

Answer (D) is incorrect because of the same notion of "newsworthiness" mentioned above with respect to answer (B). Neither the ex-lover nor Infotainment Tonite would be liable to Hilda-May for appropriation of her likeness.

135. **Answer (A) is correct.** The two versions of the privacy tort that might be used here, "disclosure of private facts" and "intrusion upon seclusion," both require an invasion into the plaintiff's private space. If the video camera had entered her home surreptitiously, Benita's claim would be stronger.

     Answer (B) is incorrect because Benita associates injury — harm related to "professional disgrace" — with the disclosure.

     Answer (C) is incorrect because the television station could have been liable if it had in fact intruded into Benita's private life.

     Answer (D) is incorrect because courts do not examine the gathering and dissemination of private facts under a reasonableness standard.

136. "Appropriation" refers to the exploitation of the plaintiff's likeness or identity for commercial gain, without the plaintiff's consent. FanRagZine has made money from the identity of Gothika without her consent. This tort denies recovery to plaintiffs, however, when what defendants appropriate is "newsworthy." Gothika is a celebrity and her experiences have news value. The appropriation tort does not compel defendants to share their profits with newsworthy plaintiffs.

137.	**Answer (B) is correct.** Dan's best hope of defeating Maureen's intentional infliction of emotional distress claim is to argue that what he did was not "extreme and outrageous." This is not necessarily a winner; a jury might find that performing invasive surgery on a person without disclosing your HIV-positive status is so inappropriate as to be outrageous. But there are countervailing considerations. For one thing, Dan took steps to avoid cutting himself, which minimized the risk of transmission of the virus. Also, society does respect people's right to privacy with respect to their medical conditions. Still, Dan did place Maureen at risk, and Dan's privacy interest might have to give way when his medical condition places an unsuspecting patient at risk.

     Answer (A) is incorrect because the tort of intentional infliction of emotional distress does not require malicious intent. One need only intend to cause serious emotional distress (not present here; on the contrary, Dan hid his HIV-positive status, which would both protect his own privacy and prevent Maureen from becoming distressed) or act with reckless disregard for causing serious emotional distress (and again, his acts show care with respect to that matter, not recklessness).

     Answer (C) is incorrect because the tort does not require any physical contact. Many successful cases of intentional infliction of emotional distress involve no contact at all between the defendant and the victim.

     Answer (D) is incorrect because it is not alone a reason to deny Maureen recovery. True, there is concern about fakery, and this is part of the reason why the plaintiff must show severe emotional distress. But the possibility of fakery does not in itself defeat an otherwise valid claim.

138.	Liability of this kind is rare. Courts are not eager to extend liability for negligent infliction of emotional distress to benefit hypersensitive plaintiffs. In exceptional situations, liability would be proper: A defendant aware of the plaintiff's sensitivity who could, through reasonable care, avoid causing the plaintiff distress, might be liable for negligent infliction of emotional distress even though the plaintiff is hypersensitive. A psychotherapist-patient relationship provides an example of this potential liability.

139.	**Answer (D) is correct.** A jury is very likely to find that Doyle's act was "extreme and outrageous" in the sense that it is utterly intolerable. Even if Doyle did not want Crane to suffer serious emotional distress, but only to see it as a joke, it is hard to imagine that a jury will not view her conduct as having been undertaken with reckless disregard for causing such distress. This was not a private practical joke, and Doyle probably realized that lots of people would think Crane really was a "deadbeat parent." As such, her conduct seems reckless. In addition, Crane suffered what the facts describe as serious emotional distress.

Answer (A) is incorrect because Doyle probably acted with reckless disregard for causing serious emotional distress, as explained above. This meets the intent requirement for intentional infliction of emotional distress.

Answer (B) is incorrect because malice is not required for this tort.

Answer (C) is incorrect because bodily harm is not required when the intended victim is the one who suffered the serious emotional distress.

140. **Answer (B) is correct.** To be liable for intentional infliction of emotional distress, the defendant must have intended to cause serious emotional distress or have acted in reckless disregard for causing it. The facts state that the captain accidentally played the crash announcement. The facts do not suggest any recklessness in doing so.

Answer (A) is incorrect because, according to the "thin skull" rule, if conduct would be tortious toward a normally constituted person, one who happens to be particularly sensitive or vulnerable may still recover for his entire damages. Thus, Daphne's extra sensitivity would not assist the airline's defense.

Answer (C) is incorrect because it is difficult to argue that playing the tape was not extreme and outrageous. It is highly likely to cause extreme distress to just about any passenger.

Answer (D) is incorrect because physical injury is not an element of intentional infliction of emotional distress.

141. **Answer (D) is correct.** To prevail in an action for intentional infliction of emotional distress, Park must prove (1) that Smith's conduct was "extreme and outrageous"; (2) that Smith acted with intention to cause severe emotional distress or with reckless disregard for that consequence; and (3) that Park suffered severe emotional distress. In context, a jury might well find that Smith's conduct was "extreme and outrageous." This was an employment context, and he was Park's immediate boss. Park is unlikely to have felt free to complain directly to Smith in that situation. In addition, many courts have found that racial/ethnic slurs go beyond mere insults, and are particularly obnoxious in our society. The second element is probably satisfied even if Smith did not intend to cause severe emotional distress. At the very least, a jury is likely to find that he acted with reckless disregard for that consequence. Finally, though the facts are not clear, Park's distress might well have been severe. She felt the need to quit her job, suggesting that the situation was particularly difficult for her.

Answer (A) is incorrect because the facts reveal that Smith believed he was promoting employee morale. Thus, the "motive" test for scope of employment seems to be satisfied.

Answer (B) is incorrect because most courts do not require proof of physical injury in actions for intentional infliction of emotional distress.

Answer (C) is incorrect because, as discussed above, Smith's actions probably satisfy the standard for recklessness, which is sufficient for this tort.

142. The oldest cases upheld liability for "fright and shock" associated with nearby trauma. Liability for this type of injury continues but now amounts to a small portion of the total. Among the emotional consequences that can be compensated are anguish (of relatives located near the body of a person who suffers physical impact, for instance), fear (of becoming ill in the future, sometimes compensable when the plaintiff has been exposed to a hazardous substance), anxiety (if sufficiently severe), deep revulsion (caused by negligent mishandling of corpses, for instance). One might also include consortium, which covers harm to familial intimacy.

143. **Answer (A) is correct.** All the elements of intentional infliction of emotional distress appear to be satisfied. Robbing a bank at gunpoint is undoubtedly "extreme and outrageous" conduct. The success of Derek's plan required the cooperation of all employees and customers, and that cooperation turned on compliance with his orders. Thus, he intended to create the kind of severe distress that led people to comply. And Cosmo's distress appears to have been severe.

Answer (B) is incorrect because the fact that a set of facts might give rise to two torts does not mean that if the statute has run on one, the other claim is barred. In addition, there is no rule requiring a party to sue only under the primary or strongest claim supported by the facts. Thus, even if Cosmo has a stronger claim for assault than for intentional infliction of emotional distress (which might not be true in any event), Cosmo's emotional distress action is not barred.

Answer (C) is incorrect because Cosmo was one of the people toward whom Derek aimed his conduct.

Answer (D) is incorrect because there is no double jeopardy problem with a crime victim's civil suit against the convicted criminal.

144. **Answer (A) is correct.** Though Parker appears to have suffered severe emotional distress, and though Dawn probably intended to cause at least some embarrassment, this kind of behavior is sufficiently common among 7th graders that it probably does not rise to the level of "extreme and outrageous."

Answer (B) is incorrect because intent to injure is not an element of intentional infliction of emotional distress. The element is intent to create severe emotional distress.

Answer (C) is incorrect because assumption of risk is not a defense to the tort of intentional infliction of emotional distress. In addition, even if it were a defense, it is not at all clear that prior acts of kidding around constituted a form of consent to this sort of conduct on Dawn's part.

Answer (D) is incorrect for the reasons stated above.

145.   **Answer (C) is correct.** Because Diego did not know that Paddy was close friends with Ronald and his wife, it appears that Diego neither intended to cause Paddy severe emotional distress nor acted with reckless disregard. According to *Restatement (Second) of Torts* § 46, someone other than the intended target of the defendant's behavior may only recover if the person is present at the time of the conduct and was either a member of the target's immediate family or suffered bodily injury. Though Paddy suffered severe emotional distress, the facts do not indicate that he suffered any bodily injury.

Answer (A) is incorrect because, as explained above, Paddy's claim appears weak.

Answer (B) is incorrect because there is little doubt that a jury will consider this sort of behavior "extreme and outrageous." Telling a person a knowingly false story that his spouse has been in an accident and probably will not survive is a truly horrible thing.

Answer (D) is incorrect because reasonable foreseeability of harm to a bystander is not an element of intentional infliction of emotional distress. The bystander element is discussed above.

146.   **Answer (A) is correct.** The most common test, sometimes called the "zone of danger" test, is incorporated in *Restatement (Second) of Torts* § 313(2), which provides that one may not recover for "emotional distress arising solely from harm or peril to a third person, unless the negligence of the actor has otherwise created an unreasonable risk of bodily harm to the other." From the facts, it does not appear that the employee created an unreasonable risk of bodily harm to Pauline. She was behind a thick glass window.

Answer (B) is incorrect because the "impact" rule required the plaintiff to have suffered some physical injury from impact. Pauline did not suffer impact, so her claim would fail under that test.

Answer (C) is incorrect because at least one type of test, represented by Dillon v. Legg, 441 P.2d 912 (Cal. 1968), *Thing v. La Chusa*, 771 P.2d 814 (Cal. 1989), and other cases, allows a bystander to recover even if the bystander was not in the "zone of danger" of physical impact.

Answer (D) is incorrect because, as explained above, Pauline will lose under several theories.

147. **Answer (C) is correct.** Because the employee's negligent handling of the equipment was a cause in fact and proximate cause of Peter's bodily injury, he may recover for that injury in a simple negligence action. When emotional distress occurs as a result of the same event that caused bodily harm to the plaintiff, all courts allow recovery of damages for emotional distress as "parasitic" to the damages for bodily harm. Because the same incident that caused Peter's bodily injury also caused the injury to Padua, Peter may recover for the emotional distress he suffered.

   Answer (A) is incorrect because Peter's recovery for his own bodily injury does not depend on whether he observed his son's impaling by the equipment. Also, for the reasons stated above, Peter may recover for emotional distress.

   Answer (B) is incorrect because the foreseeability of emotional distress does not matter when there is liability for physical injury. In addition, in all likelihood emotional distress *is* a reasonably foreseeable outcome of the kind of accident caused by the employee's negligence.

   Answer (D) is incorrect because, as discussed above, the jurisdiction's test for negligent infliction of emotional distress will not affect Peter's recovery in this situation.

148. **Answer (B) is correct.** Because there was no physical impact, Peter does not satisfy the "impact" test. However, the jury will probably find that he was in the zone of danger from the negligent handling of the equipment because, as an occupant of the car, he, too, was a reasonably foreseeable victim of the negligent handling of the equipment.

   Answers (A) and (D) are incorrect for the reasons just stated.

   Answer (C) is incorrect because even if Peter did not have sensory awareness of the injury to Padua as it was happening, Peter was in the zone of danger created by the negligent handling of the equipment. Where the zone of danger test is satisfied, courts using *Dillon*-type tests would allow plaintiff to recover. *See Dillon v. Legg*, 441 P.2d 912 (Cal. 1968)

149. Perry's claim is for fear of contracting disease as a result of the hospital's negligence. There is little doubt that Perry's anxiety and distress are real. The problem is that Perry did not actually contract the disease. In this situation, different jurisdictions reach different results. Some courts would deny recovery altogether, largely on the ground that to allow recovery would open the courts to a flood of litigation. Other courts would allow Perry to recover as long as she can prove that she actually was exposed to the virus. In those jurisdictions, proof that the blood contained the virus and that some blood got into Perry's system probably would suffice. Some courts would allow recovery even absent proof of actual exposure. Regardless of the general approach, courts generally limit recovery to the period of anxiety before Perry learned that she was not infected.

150. **Answer (D) is correct.** Many jurisdictions permit recovery for negligent infliction of emotional distress based on this fact pattern. Some require physical injury, but Glenda's loss of sleep, headaches, and stomach pain probably suffice. Courts that allow recovery do not apply the same tests used for cases in which a bystander suffers distress at the negligent injury to another person. They view the plaintiff as a reasonably foreseeable victim of the defendant's negligence, and thus hold that a duty of reasonable care is owed to the plaintiff.

Answer (A) is incorrect because it does not matter that Glenda did not observe the negligent addressing of the telegram.

Answer (B) is incorrect because, as stated above, courts do not apply the same tests applicable to the bystander recovery cases.

Answer (C) is incorrect because a normal person in Glenda's position probably would suffer meaningful emotional distress, and perhaps physical illness as well. Even if Glenda's reaction was somewhat greater than what the average person would experience, the "thin skull" rule would apply to the situation, and she would be able to recover for the full extent of her harm.

151. **Answer (B) is correct.** The Hoof & Mouth partners fulfilled the elements of the tort of fraud (or intentional misrepresentation).

      Answer (A) is incorrect because it does not state a correct rule of law. Hoof & Mouth is a wrongdoer.

      Answer (C) is incorrect. Although it may be true, it does not explain why Metrobank should prevail.

      Answer (D) is incorrect. The "representation of Regiment" was not unlawful; the fraudulent behaviors of Regiment and Hoof & Mouth were unlawful.

152. **Answer (A) is correct.** It is usually hard to know or predict the consequences of a false statement. If ignorance about the consequences was sufficient to defeat the claim, most of the tort would disappear.

      Answer (B) is incorrect. Knowledge that the statement made was false is a crucial element of intentional (as contrasted with negligent) misrepresentation.

      Answers (C) and (D) are incorrect. Most courts consider Answers (C) and (D) to be crucial elements of the tort as well.

153. **Answer (C) is correct.** The statement is accurate, and it explains the rule of no liability in this situation.

      Answer (A) is incorrect. Answer (A) establishes the negligence of the defendant, which may well be a correct conclusion. But when the financial consequences of negligence to the plaintiff are only lost benefits or opportunities pursuant to a contract, these losses are not recoverable.

      Answer (B) is incorrect. Answer (B), like Answer (A), may well be true but does not suffice to support the claim.

      Answer (D) is incorrect. The answer is somewhat obscure, but seems to assert that the plaintiff's losses are covered by contract. This conclusion has no support in the facts.

154. **Answer (C) is correct.** Dolly was both a liar and a careless businessperson: She committed both the intentional and the negligent versions of the misrepresentation tort. When the bank official asked Dolly whether she had personally chosen the accounting firm and Dolly said yes, she made a false statement — and it is fair to infer that the statement was material (at an interview, the questions frequently matter to the questioner) and that it induced

reliance. Thus the elements of the intentional tort are satisfied. Regarding negligent misrepresentation, the problem says that Dolly sincerely believed her net worth to be more like $10 million rather than less than $1 million, suggesting she probably assumed that the crony's "audited financial statement" was accurate, or close to accurate, and also that she was careless to hold this belief and not verify what Madison gave her before submitting it as part of a loan application.

Answers (A), (B), and (D) are incorrect because under these facts, both intentional and negligent misrepresentation are available claims.

155.   **Answer (D) is correct.** Louisa seems to be a cheater whose dumb cheating cost her partner money, but she did not commit a tort against her partner. She made the misrepresentation (tampering with the offer document) to the seller, not to Bonnie Blue. The only contracts she interfered with were (in part) her own, and a defendant cannot be liable for tortious interference with her own contractual relations.

Answers (A), (B), and (C) are incorrect because under these facts, both misrepresentation and tortious interference with contract are *not* available to Bonnie Blue.

156.   The former tort claim requires an existing, enforceable contract; the latter does not. Courts agree that the prerogative to interfere with another person's business is stronger when the interest at stake is mere "opportunity" rather than the more definite, fixed "contract." In the infamous case of Texaco, Inc. v. Pennzoil Co., 729 S.W. 2d 768 (Tex. App. 1987), the court made a crucial ruling that an agreement intended to lead to a future merger constituted a "contract," thus putting the plaintiff, Pennzoil, in a much stronger position to recover.

157.   **Answer (D) is correct.** The topic here is *spoliation*: the destruction of evidence necessary to pursue a claim. Most jurisdictions do not provide a tort remedy for spoliation. One exception to the no-liability stance is something like a bailment-like contract between the plaintiff and the defendant to take care of the physical evidence.

Answer (A) is incorrect. It is belied by the facts. We have seen nothing to suggest that Timeshare assumed a duty of care.

Answer (B) is incorrect. It is obscure. A defendant that has "exceeded the scope of its employment" has done nothing to incur tort liability. We would need to know something more, and having "caused financial loss" is not enough.

Answer (C) is incorrect. It is irrelevant to a spoliation claim.

158.   **Answer (A) is correct.** Although the question is written at a rather theoretical plane, it ought to be clear that Answer (A) is different from the other choices. Answers (B), (C), and (D) all militate *in favor* of liability for economic loss. Answer (A)'s point about "nearly infinite

chain reactions" suggests that courts have a difficult time administering liability for economic loss. This administrative difficulty is an argument against liability.

Answers (B), (C), and (D) are incorrect for the reasons just given.

159. **Answer (B) is correct.** Of all the choices, Answer (B) eliminates fault and negligence the most decisively. In Answer (B), the defendant behaved as carefully as he could. In general, courts disfavor strict liability for misrepresentation. Violations of labeling statutes constitute one of the few vital corners of this tort.

Answer (A) is incorrect. While Genevieve also seems not to be at fault, she probably did not make a misrepresentation. She said something like, "According to this map that I have had commissioned, my land has unobstructed access to a lake." That statement appears to be true. There is no suggestion of her withholding any material information from Barton, nor of her intending to induce reliance.

Answers (C) and (D) are incorrect because both showcase careless persons, neither of whom would be strictly liable. In Answer (C), Dalma appears to have committed negligent misrepresentation when she presented financial statements prepared by an auditor whom she knew to be dubious. Answer (D), like Answer (B), probably contains no misrepresentation of any kind. Instead, this is an instance of an ignorant buyer meeting an ignorant seller.

160. Yes, S is wrong. Although the plaintiff will often have a claim against the breaching party (for breach of contract), she need not pursue it in order to bring a claim against the interferer. Courts regard the two actions as separate and independent.

161. **Answer (B) is correct.** Courts agree that contributory or comparative negligence is available in legal malpractice claims, just as it is available in medical malpractice claims — that is to say, sparingly applied, because of the heightened duty of care that the professional holds, but not categorically precluded either.

Answer (A) is incorrect because it categorically precludes consideration of Carmen's behavior, and that is wrong.

Answer (C) is incorrect because it brings in an irrelevant reference to causation in fact, which is usually part of the plaintiff's case, not the defendant's.

Answer (D) is incorrect because it is both factually and legally dubious. The wording of the problem suggests that Llewellyn had several other opportunities to catch the error after Carmen missed it. As a statement of law it is equally wrong; "last clear chance" is a doctrine used against defendants (to soften the harsh effects of contributory negligence), and does not limit a plaintiff's opportunity to recover.

162. Courts are divided on this issue, but several cases recognize claims for emotional and reputational harm. They usually require that the emotional or reputational harm be foreseeable. One type of tortious interference with contract that seems well suited to this kind of damages award is the unlawful obstruction of an employment contract. The supporting rationale is that the claim is one of tort, and tort law recognizes these interests. The contrary rationale is that the claim is linked to a contract, and contract law does not generally recognize these interests.

163. **Answer (D) is correct.** Damages for a death caused by negligence may include such things as future earnings, but if the person's expected lifetime was already likely to be shorter than average, it is not appropriate to calculate damages based on figures for an average lifetime. Thus, damages for Arni's death must take into account the likelihood that he would have died earlier than an average person.

Answer (A) is incorrect because it misconceives the "thin skull" rule. Under that rule, a defendant may not defend the action on the basis of the plaintiff's extra sensitivity. *If* the defendant's behavior would have caused harm to a healthy person, then defendant is liable for the full damages suffered by a person whose health made her particularly susceptible to harm from defendant's activity. Arni fell into this class. His weakened immune system was more affected than that of the average person, but as the facts show, many people (including, presumably, otherwise healthy people) were injured by the contaminated water. Their injuries were not permanent, but they were harmed nonetheless.

Answer (B) is incorrect because the facts make clear that the contaminated water was a cause in fact of Arni's death. Other factors (such as the weakened immune system caused by the AIDS virus) were also causes, but this does not mean the water contamination was not a cause.

Answer (C) is incorrect because Arni did in fact suffer damage. His life was shortened even more than it would have been as a result of the AIDS virus.

164. Because punitive damage awards are noncompensatory, some observers believe there is no good reason for the plaintiff to keep them. In principle, compensatory damages rectify her injury. Other observers favor disallowing plaintiffs from retaining punitive damages awards in the belief that tort judgments are simply too high, and need to be reduced before adverse, hard-to-reverse social consequences ensue. The contrary stance urges that plaintiffs be allowed to keep their punitive damages awards on the ground that even though in principle the plaintiff does not "need" or "deserve" these sums, the defendant "needs" or "deserves" punishment. If plaintiffs could not collect punitive damages, they would be less willing to bring claims, and defendants would enjoy a windfall. Others argue that punitive damages help to compensate for the percentage of recovery that the plaintiff turns over to her lawyer as a fee.

If punitive damages are to be taken from the plaintiff, one might argue that the most appropriate public purpose would address one of two general categories: the awards should go to either (A) some tort-like need, such as compensation for personal injuries inflicted by insolvent defendants or perhaps for health insurance, or to (B) a public need that cannot be met adequately through taxation, perhaps to benefit a politically unpopular but deserving class. An alternative approach would simply turn the money over to the state treasury as general revenue.

165. **Answer (A) is correct.** Courts have long permitted awards for emotional distress as "parasitic" to the physical harm that is a prerequisite for a negligence claim. Here, the car was damaged, so Preston may recover for emotional distress, if he can prove it occurred.

Answer (B) is incorrect because it assumes damages are limited to those that are reasonably foreseeable. That is not the correct rule.

Answer (C) is incorrect because it assumes that the restrictions on causes of action for negligent infliction of emotional distress apply here. This is not, however, a claim for negligent infliction of emotional distress. As explained above, Preston is simply seeking emotional distress damages in his regular negligence claim.

Answer (D) is incorrect because it does not take account of the "thin skull" rule. If a defendant's behavior created an unreasonable risk of harm to a normally constituted person (and that would be true here, where Doe struck Preston's car repeatedly), the plaintiff may recover all of the harm he actually suffers, even if some of it results from a preexisting condition that makes him more vulnerable than most people.

166. **Answer (C) is correct.** The purpose of discounting damages to present value is to prevent a plaintiff from collecting more than she would have collected if she had not been injured. Lost future earnings relate to income that the plaintiff would have collected in the future, without an injury. Because she would not have received all of this income at the time of judgment, she would be overcompensated if she received it all at this point. She'd get to invest it and collect not only the principal but interest.

Answer (A) is incorrect because the collateral source rule is unrelated to this question. It refers to additional sources of compensation.

Answer (B) is incorrect because damages for past pain and suffering are fully realized at the time of judgment; they have no "future," and only future losses are subject to discounting to present value.

Answer (D) is incorrect because the purpose of punitive damages is not compensatory, and not closely related to the plaintiff's future losses. Punitive damages are set at an amount to punish and motivate the defendant.

167. **Answer (A) is correct.** Wrongful formation claims seek the expenses of pregnancy and childbirth, and sometimes for child rearing. Typically a plaintiff cannot reduce these costs after wrongful formation occurs. When childrearing expenses are sought, the way to mitigate the harm is either by relinquishing the baby for adoption or terminating the pregnancy.

Courts generally view these measures as too burdensome. Such options are available to prospective parents before negligent sterilization occurs; the reason they chose sterilization was to avoid going through the measures.

Answers (B), (C), and (D) are incorrect because although mitigation is not always possible, scenarios can arise under all of them where the plaintiff has an opportunity to lower the cost of the injury through reasonable conduct.

168. The collateral source rule, a common law doctrine, provides that damages are not reduced by the amount of benefits that a plaintiff receives from other sources to help deal with the injury. For example, if the plaintiff received money for rehabilitative treatment from a health insurance provider, the defendant will not be allowed to subtract these sums from the total of damages to reflect this compensation. The plaintiff may well end up with a 'double recovery' for such benefits. To avoid jeopardizing the plaintiff's entitlements, the collateral source rule further provides that the defendant may not introduce evidence of these benefits at trial. Some states have modified the collateral rule by statute, especially for medical malpractice claims.

169. **Answer (D) is correct.** It may be helpful to think of a numerator and a denominator. Caps on damages address the denominator (the total amounts of judgments and settlements), not the numerator (the percentage of a judgment or settlement that the lawyer would collect as a fee). The problem in Answer (D) is one of finding the right percentage to pay a lawyer — a 'numerator' problem, if you will, rather than a denominator problem. Thus it does not relate closely to the 'denominator' concern of the question.

Answer (A) is incorrect because a wide range of recoverable damages makes the pricing of insurance more difficult.

Answer (B) is incorrect because if the amount that a plaintiff can recover is unlimited, a personal injury lawyer is more likely to file a weak claim than would be the case if recovery is limited.

Answer (C) is incorrect because the risk of paying high damages affects the profitability of products sold in the market. This threat to profits might induce a manufacturer not to offer a product for sale.

170. **Answer (B) is correct**. The three criteria mentioned are the ones provided in the *BMW* decision, and they are met under these facts.

Answer (A) is incorrect because the *BMW* decision does not discuss actual malice. A similar concept is included in the reprehensibility criterion, but "actual malice" is a term of art not used here.

Answer (C) is incorrect because there is no separate rule for personal injury cases. (Ira Gore, the plaintiff in *BMW of North America Inc. v. Gore*, suffered only economic loss based on property damage.)

Answer (D) is incorrect because punitive damages claims are not preempted by "lemon laws."

171. This argument, sometimes called the "per diem" approach, has been disapproved by some judges and permitted by others. *Pro*: It expresses pain and suffering in relatively concrete, specific terms. It reminds the jury that the plaintiff will not live forever, possibly placing a cap on reckless excess. Although it is far from ideal, if rigid specificity is required, future pain and suffering would be impossible to recognize in terms of money damages, and under non-recognition would unfairly enrich defendants. *Con*: It is imprecise and encourages false quantification. It is inaccurate in that the 'curve' of suffering is probably not linear: victims will often experience intense distress at first, then adjust somewhat. It might inflame the jury into an exaggerated measure of damages.

172. **Answer (B) is correct.** It presents a claim for trespass to land, the cause of action where courts are most receptive to an award of nominal damages.

Answer (A) is incorrect because it suggests carelessness on the part of Empire, not actual malice, generally understood to mean an intentional lie or reckless disregard of the truth. As a public figure, Estevez could not recover in this defamation claim without proving actual malice.

Answer (C) is incorrect because it is a claim for nuisance, which requires actual damages.

Answer (D) is incorrect because it is a claim for negligent infliction of emotional distress, which requires actual damages.

173. **Answer (A) is correct.** Under the doctrine of joint and several liability, each negligent defendant is responsible for the full amount of the judgment. The judgment, however, must reflect a reduction of the plaintiff's damages in accordance with the plaintiff's own fault. Here, if Ermintrude's fault was 35% of the total, and she suffered $10,000 of damages, she can only recover $6500. She will receive a judgment in that amount against both Ludwig's and Needlenose, and may recover that amount (and no more) from one of the defendants or a combination of the two.

     Answer (B) is incorrect because joint and several liability allows Ermintrude to receive a judgment for the full amount against both defendants (even though her recovery will be limited to $6500 in total).

     Answer (C) is incorrect because Ermintrude's judgment must be reduced according to the degree of her own fault.

     Answer (D) is incorrect because, under a pure system of comparative fault, a plaintiff may recover even against a defendant whose negligence was less than plaintiff's.

174. Respondeat superior, which is liability imposed on employers for those torts of their employees that are within the scope of the employees' employment. This liability has been described as "strict," meaning that the plaintiff need not prove fault on the part of the employer. Respondeat superior does not transfer liability away from the employee. She too is liable for her own torts; she and the employer are jointly and severally liable to those she injures in the scope of her employment.

175. **Answer (A) is correct.** A passenger is not vicariously liable for the actions of her driver unless the driver was the passenger's agent. Bender was not Fry's agent. Unless Hermes can prove that Fry negligently contributed to Bender's loss of concentration, Hermes may not recover against Fry.

     Answer (B) is incorrect because this type of joint venture does not impose vicarious liability on the passenger. Vicarious liability might be imposed if Bender and Fry had been involved in a business outing, but they were just sharing a ride to a park to play basketball with friends.

     Answer (C) is incorrect because Fry's possible awareness of Bender's bad driving skills does not make Fry liable to a third party in the event Bender causes harm. The fact might affect Fry's own recovery against Bender, but that is not the issue here.

Answer (D) is incorrect because it does not provide a reason for imposing liability on a non-negligent party. Again, Fry was not the person who acted negligently.

176. Contribution refers to the sharing of liability between two or more defendants. A defendant who pays more than its rightful share of a judgment can seek contribution from other responsible defendants, either in a separate lawsuit or by bringing a third-party action as part of the plaintiff's suit. Indemnity refers to full repayment of damages to the defendant who has paid them. It is generally created by contract.

177. **Answer (C) is correct.** Zoid will be liable for the back injury because it was caused by her own negligence. Hiram will be liable because his original negligence in causing the accident was a cause in fact and proximate cause of the back injury. Courts hold almost unanimously that a tortfeasor is liable for enhanced injury caused by a rescuer, medical personnel, or others who render aid to the victim. Under a "directness" or "intervening cause" theory of proximate cause, the doctor is not treated as a "superseding cause." Under a scope of risk analysis, additional harm suffered at the hands of a rescuer or medical personnel is within the foreseeable scope of risk created by the original act of negligence. (Some courts explain that the harm was within the scope of risk by noting that the dust had not yet settled from the original accident when Stingray suffered further injury.)

Answers (A) and (B) are incorrect because, as explained above, both Bender and Zoid are liable for the back injury.

Answer (D) is incorrect because there is no need to apportion responsibility for the back injury; both Hiram and Zoid will be liable for the full injury (though Stingray may not recover more than the amount of that injury). This is a situation in which the court will impose joint and several liability.

178. **Answer (D) is correct.** This is *not* a case of nonfeasance, where the plaintiff seeks to hold a party responsible for failure to prevent harm. Here, the action asserts that the father actively contributed to his son's eventual violence. If the research is correct, the father's beatings might have been a cause in fact of the later harm because they increased the son's tendency toward violence. This might be difficult to prove, and the son's own criminal conduct (the murders) might be viewed as beyond the scope of the father's responsibility, but the mere fact that the father was not directly involved in the murder will not absolve him of responsibility.

Answer (A) is incorrect because the plaintiff's theory is not that the father failed to control the conduct of his child. As explained above, the theory is that the father actively contributed to the child's violent tendencies.

Answer (B) is incorrect because plaintiff's theory is not one of vicarious liability.

Answer (C) is incorrect because it cannot be said as a matter of law that the son's criminal behavior "broke the chain," absolving the father of responsibility. Courts hold that even a criminal actor's conduct does not necessarily supersede, especially if it is reasonably foreseeable. There is probably a jury question here as to the father's responsibility.

179. Both respondeat superior and strict products liability are forms of "enterprise liability," generally understood to mean strict liability of business enterprises for the harms that their activity causes as part of "doing business." Both types of liability are paid for by customers of the business, in a kind of insurance. The overlap between the set of customers and the set of plaintiffs is usually stronger in products liability than respondeat superior — especially when the product is one devised for individual consumers — but both doctrines spread costs to a customer base in order to compensate injured persons and create incentives to safety.

180. **Answer (A) is correct**. Darren is not vicariously liable for Endora's attack. Endora was not Darren's agent. To be liable to Jade, Darren must have been negligent in some respect, probably in supervising the residents to prevent them from doing things such as this.

Answer (B) is incorrect for the reasons just given.

Answer (C) is incorrect because, even if Darren negligently supervised the residents, he might be liable for Endora's conduct. The reason is that Endora's attack on Jade is one of the things Darren's supervision is designed to prevent.

Answer (D) is incorrect because the facts simply do not support the conclusion that Darren "permitted" Endora to escape. Perhaps other evidence will provide support for this conclusion, but facts given in the problem do not.

181. **Answer (D) is correct.** The presence or absence of comparative fault in a particular case is a separate question that does not pertain directly to the debate over whether to retain or abolish joint and several liability. The other arguments are frequently mentioned by critics.

Answer (A) is incorrect because it argues that the arrival of comparative fault (as a doctrine, not in a particular case) has made courts and juries familiar with fractional apportionment, and so it makes sense to apply this practice toward "proportional," rather than joint and several, liability.

Answer (B) is incorrect. It is a fairness argument that critics often raise.

Answer (C) is incorrect. This argument comes up frequently in the context of workplace injury, where an employer is much more to blame than a product manufacturer, but because of employer immunity, the product manufacturer is saddled with the worker's damages.

182. **Answer (B) is correct.** If Mugwump weren't insolvent, the damages would be awarded as follows: Orestes $400,000, Billiard $300,000, Mugwump $200,000, and Wallawalla

$100,000. Under Cranberry law, Tyler should receive the full $1,000,000 in damages. The Mugwump shortfall means that the other three defendants have to make up the share that Mugwump would have paid.

The calculation can be explained in different ways. Here is one method: The ratio of liability among Orestes, Billiard, and Wallawalla assigned by the jury is 4:3:1. That is, in the new post-Mugwump distribution, Billiard should be paying three times as much as Wallawalla, and Orestes should be paying four times as much as Wallawalla. The total amount of money to be paid is $1,000,000.

Or, algebraically: $4x + 3x + 2x + x = \$1,000,000$.

Thus, $8x = \$1,000,000$.

And then, $x = \$125,000$.

Wallawalla pays x ($125,000). Billiard pays $3x$ ($375,000). Orestes pays $4x$ ($500,000).

Answer (A) is incorrect because it ignores the fact that Mugwump is insolvent.

Answer (C) is incorrect because it deprives Tyler of the missing $200,000, a result that Cranberry law rejects.

Answer (D) is incorrect because it seems to be imposing an additional 20% on each remaining defendant, for no particular reason. Close (i.e. 96% of the proper total sum), but no cigar.

183. Jury. The question is typically fact-specific. Unfortunately for employers, scope-of-employment disputes often cannot be resolved in summary judgment proceedings.

184. Parents are liable for the torts of their children when the parents were at fault: for example, when they fail to control a dangerous child. (Note that this liability is usually imposed only when the parents knew about the dangerousness of the child and had the ability to control him or her.) They can be liable under ordinary principles of vicarious liability: when they employed the child and the child committed a tort in the scope of his employment, or when they were in partnership with the child and the child committed a tort pursuant to the activities of the partnership. Some states hold them liable by statute as owners of a motor vehicle that the child drives negligently.

PRACTICE FINAL EXAM: ANSWERS

185. **Answer (D) is correct.** A victim of negligence who acts out of a desire for self-preservation, and in the course of doing so suffers further harm, is not viewed as a superseding cause that ends the wrongdoer's liability even if the victim's conduct, viewed in the context of the emergency situation, is negligent. However, if the jury believes that the victim acted unreasonably (even given the exigent circumstances), the jury may reduce the victim's recovery according to the jurisdiction's comparative fault rules.

Answer (C) is incorrect because it assumes that contributory negligence will have no effect on Pearl's recovery.

Answer (A) is incorrect because it assumes that the victim's effort at self-preservation will be a superseding cause of her harm. This is contrary to the law as discussed above.

Answer (B) is incorrect for the same reason as Answer (A) and because it wrongly suggests that the emergency circumstances may not be taken into account in judging the reasonableness of Pearl's actions.

186. **Answer (A) is correct.** Winkle's case fails on the cause in fact element. Very likely, the fire started by Rocky *would have* destroyed Winke's house if it had been there, but the Whatsamatta U fire got there first. Thus, Rocky's fire did not harm Winkle.

Answer (B) is incorrect because it doesn't matter what Rocky's fire would have done. We already know that it did not, in fact, burn down Winkle's house.

Answer (C) is incorrect because it assumes that a party who has breached a duty of reasonable care is liable even if other elements of the cause of action are not satisfied. The nature of a cause of action is otherwise: all elements must be met, or the action fails completely.

Answer (D) is incorrect because Whatsamatta U's insolvency, while unfortunate, does not give Winkle a valid claim against a party who did not cause Winkle harm. The same is true for the fact that Winkle is innocent. True, the outcome will be that Winkle will have no one from whom to recover, but that is not sufficient to make another party responsible in the absence of a valid cause of action against that party.

187. **Answer (C) is correct.** Manu was privileged by the doctrine of necessity to go onto Pam's land to try to prevent further harm. That means Manu did not commit trespass, even though it entered the land intentionally. However, courts treat the necessity doctrine as creating a limited privilege. The person is not a trespasser, but must pay for damage caused.

Answer (A) is incorrect because, as noted, Manu's privilege made its entry not a trespass.

Answer (B) is incorrect because the situation did not come about as a result of any *fault* on Manu's part. The facts make clear that Manu's employee did not handle the drum negligently. The doctrine of necessity applies.

Answer (D) is incorrect because, as noted above, the person who enters the land of another out of necessity must pay for damages caused, even if the person was not a trespasser.

188. **Answer (B) is correct.** The issue here is whether Gary performed the surgery in accordance with the applicable standard of care. That makes it a negligence case, and it appears to be strong because the facts indicate that he used too large a tube, and that it caused permanent damage.

Answer (A) is incorrect because the surgery, even if negligently performed and even if it took place against Carla's wishes, was not an unconsented contact. Carla is too young to give consent to surgery. Her parents have that responsibility, and they made their decision after learning the nature of the surgery.

Answer (C) is incorrect because, even if Carla did suffer apprehension of imminent harmful or offensive contact, her apprehension was not caused by any unlawful act of Gary. She may have been apprehensive, but that stemmed from the prospect of surgery to which her parents lawfully consented.

Answer (D) is incorrect because, as indicated above, Carla appears to have a strong negligence case against Gary.

189. **Answer (C) is correct.** The issue here is one of duty. Adam is a trespasser. Although he was legally on campus, this fenced-off part of the campus no doubt was out of bounds for students. At common law, a possessor of land owed no duty of reasonable care toward a trespasser. (Most states held that there was only a duty to refrain from willful and wanton conduct toward trespassers; this case involved only a condition on the property, and no overt conduct that harmed Adam.)

Answer (A) is incorrect because it assumes a duty was owed.

Answer (B) is incorrect because any negligence by Wynona (here, leaving the mixer where the wind could blow it and the cable could snap) was a "but-for" cause of Adam's injury.

Answer (D) is incorrect because we have sufficient facts to decide the duty question at common law.

Note that the issue of "attractive nuisance" does not arise here because Adam was not a child.

190. **Answer (D) is correct.** If the common law rule limiting the duty of land possessors toward trespassers has been abolished, the possessor will owe a general duty of reasonable care regardless of the entrant's status. Satisfying that duty, however, requires a close look at the circumstances of the case. Here, we are not provided with sufficient information to judge the reasonableness of leaving a cement mixer suspended in the air at this site. It is not uncommon for contractors to suspend valuable equipment when the site is shut down, but there are some situations in which doing so poses an unreasonable danger. This might be one of them, but we can't tell without more facts.

Answer (A) is incorrect because, as indicated above, the reasonableness of Wynona's acts cannot be determined without more facts.

Answer (B) is incorrect because any negligence on Wynona's part was a "but-for" cause of Adam's injury.

Answer (C) is incorrect because Wynona did owe Adam a duty of reasonable care.

191. Negligent infliction of emotional distress. Drucilla's conduct toward the psychiatrist was merely negligent. Because the facts do not reveal that Walrus suffered physical harm, a typical negligence action is not cognizable, but an action for negligent infliction of emotional distress might be. Cases involving mistaken identity have traditionally qualified, albeit in different contexts. For example, a telegraph company that sends a telegram notifying next-of-kin of a person's death, but directed to the wrong family, can be held liable for negligent infliction of emotional distress. And a funeral home that places the wrong body in the casket for an open casket funeral has also been held liable. The present situation seems analogous because it also involves mistaken identity and also is the type of situation that is likely to cause very real emotional distress — in this situation, embarrassment and humiliation.

Intentional infliction of emotional distress does not suit the facts for at least three reasons. First, as to psychiatrist Walrus, Drucilla's conduct was negligent, not intentional. Second, even if Drucilla acted with the intent to cause serious emotional distress in the other Walrus (which might well have been her purpose — to induce him to catch up on his child support payments), her intent to cause such distress was probably not unlawful. Walrus was a wrongdoer, and a jury might not view Drucilla's method (albeit a very public one) of getting him to pay up as "extreme and outrageous." Third, even if the jury views it as extreme and outrageous, courts do not treat intentional infliction of emotional distress as a "trespassory tort" that allows for application of the "transferred intent" doctrine except in situations in which an unintended victim, present when the act occurs, suffers physical harm in addition to emotional distress. *See Restatement (Second) of Torts* § 46. Because psychiatrist Crane did not suffer physical harm, he may not recover for intentional infliction of emotional distress.

192.   **Answer (A) is correct.** In addition to proving duty and breach (which the problem asks us to assume), plaintiff must carry the burden of proving cause in fact and proximate cause.

Answer (B) is incorrect because it assumes Norm assumes the risk of harm from a cell phone user as a matter of primary assumption of risk. This is not the type of situation in which primary assumption of risk will likely apply. Drivers are entitled to assume that other drivers will act reasonably; they do not impliedly consent to negligent driving merely by taking to the road. This is not like a sports contest in which plaintiff and defendant are participants, or in which one pays to observe the other participating.

Answer (C) is incorrect because courts do not treat possession of more information about causation as, in itself, a sufficient reason to shift burden of proof on causation to the defendant. Something more is needed, such as the existence of two tortfeasors who cause an indivisible harm, or of two tortfeasors who have both breached a duty of care toward the plaintiff, but only one of whom caused the harm. Neither situation exists here.

Answer (D) is incorrect because the fact that use of a cell phone while driving is legal is not, in itself, sufficient to immunize the defendant from liability for negligence. A person in compliance with the law may still be found negligent. In other words, while *violation* of certain statutes is negligence per se, *compliance* is rarely reasonable care per se.

193.   Richards, for whose acts the city will be vicariously liable, undertook to advise Demetria about her options. Though he told Demetria about the witness protection program, he left out some very important facts about Frank's dangerousness that might have led Demetria to enter the program. By his acts, Frank arguably created a special relationship, and thus had a duty to act reasonably for her safety.

194.   **Answer (C) is correct.** The question of breach is left to the jury unless a reasonable jury could reach only one conclusion. Here, on the given facts, it is not absolutely clear that the city's confinement of Frank satisfied its duty of reasonable care to Demetria. That appears likely, but it is not so clear that the judge should take the case away from the jury.

Answers (A) and (B) are incorrect because, as explained above, the breach issue is not so clear.

Answer (D) is incorrect because none of the rationales for burden shifting apply here.

195.   **Answer (D) is correct.** The only form of assumption of risk that might have any application in a fact pattern such as this is the "secondary" form, which requires the voluntary confrontation of a known and appreciated hazard. Had Demetria been warned that she would be murdered at the bus stop, and had she gone there despite the warning, assumption of risk

might apply. But here, she received a warning about the consequences of testifying, something that had not yet happened. The facts clearly show that she did not confront a specific hazard about which she knew. The court should therefore decide the question as a matter of law.

Answer (A) is incorrect because this would not be a case of "primary" assumption of risk. Demetria was not involved in an activity with the killers such as a sporting event. Thus, it would make no sense to speak of accepting hazards inherent in the activity.

Answer (B) is incorrect because, as explained above, there are no facts supporting assumption of risk in its secondary sense.

Answer (C) is incorrect because assumption of risk and contributory (comparative) negligence are separate doctrines. Whether she acted reasonably in waiting for the bus is a question to be addressed under comparative negligence, not assumption of risk. (You should be aware, however, that some courts conflate the two defenses, and hold that under a system of comparative fault, the doctrine of secondary assumption of risk disappears because it is completely subsumed by comparative negligence. This assumes that assumption of risk in its secondary sense requires unreasonable conduct — contributorily negligent conduct. That was not the case at common law. Courts would hold that a plaintiff who voluntarily confronted an appreciated hazard assumed the risk, even if their decision under the circumstances was not unreasonable.)

196. **Answer (D) is correct.** Diva appears to have run toward Pluto with the intention of creating in him the apprehension of suffering imminent harmful or offensive contact. It was unlawful for her to do this, especially when her object was to steal his concert ticket. Pluto appears to have suffered the apprehension. This is an assault.

Answer (A) is incorrect because an action may constitute both a battery and an assault. There is some overlap between the two.

Answer (B) is incorrect because "fright" is not an element of assault. Pluto need only have been "apprehensive," which means he need only have believed Diva was going to contact him harmfully or offensively.

Answer (C) is incorrect because assumption of risk is not a defense to assault. *Consent* can be a defense, but the facts do not support it. Pluto did not consent to having Diva take his concert ticket.

197. **Answer (B) is correct.** A person has a privilege to use reasonable force to protect himself from what he believes to be an imminent unlawful contact. If the jury finds that Pluto reasonably believed Diva was about to strike him, and if the jury finds that the amount of force Pluto used to repel the attack was not excessive under the circumstances, Pluto has a good self-defense claim.

Answer (A) is incorrect because whether Pluto reasonably believed Diva was going to batter him, and whether the force Pluto used was reasonable under the circumstances, are questions for the jury (unless the facts are so clear that a reasonable jury could only reach one conclusion).

Answer (C) is incorrect for two reasons. First, it fails to take account of the "reasonable mistake" aspect of self-defense. As long as Pluto's error in thinking Diva was going to strike him was reasonable, self-defense is still available to him. Second, the question is one of fact for the jury, not for the judge (unless the facts are so clear that a reasonable jury could only reach one conclusion).

Answer (D) is incorrect because, as indicated above, what matters is whether Pluto reasonably believed Diva was going to batter him, not what Diva actually believed.

198. **Answer (C) is correct.** Eliot's strongest claim is that George did not exercise the care of a reasonable person in deciding to stand up while the bus was moving. The court will allow the jury to take into account that George was elderly, because age affects one's stability and strength. While it might have been reasonable for a younger person to do what George did, it might not have been reasonable for a person of his age to do it.

Answer (A) is incorrect because it misstates the required mental state for battery and because George did not possess that mental state. It is not enough to say that George "should have realized" he was substantially certain to fall. The law of battery requires proof that George did in fact realize it. The facts do not support this conclusion.

Answer (B) is incorrect because, even if George knew he was more prone to fall than a younger person would be, this is not the same as saying he knew he would strike another person when he fell. (Of course, nothing suggests that he desired to strike another person.) The requisite intent is missing.

Answer (D) is incorrect for the reason given above. The jury should take George's age into account when deciding the reasonableness of his conduct.

199. **Answer (A) is correct.** John acted intentionally in a way that tended to deprive Kermit of a prospective economic opportunity, the chance to purchase the bakery.

Answer (B) is incorrect because the problem specifies that no contract existed between Augustine and Kermit.

Answer (C) is incorrect because the story is true.

Answer (D) is incorrect because the formal disposition of criminal charges is generally considered to be public information, whose revelation cannot generate liability for disclosure of private facts–the only branch of the privacy tort that could apply here.

200.   **Answer (D) is correct.** Under principles of vicarious liability, an employer may be liable for an employee's conduct even if that conduct violates explicit instructions. The question is whether the conduct is considered within the "scope" of employment. Different tests are used to decide that question. Some courts apply the *Restatement of Agency* test that imposes vicarious liability for an employee's acts done out of a desire to serve the master. It is unclear whether that would be true here; stopping the bus to adjust an uncomfortable uniform does not appear to be something done with that intention. Other courts apply a foreseeability test, asking whether the negligent act or omission is a reasonably foreseeable event given the nature of the job and the circumstances. Under that test, the driver's act is much more likely to be seen as within the scope of employment, especially if drivers do this sort of thing fairly often. In all, courts tend not to place a great deal of emphasis on the fact that the act or omission was in violation of established rules or instructions. Instead, they focus more on the timing of the act (while performing a work-related job or not) and other similar factors. In all, the court is likely to hold in this case that the driver's conduct was within the scope of employment.

   Answer (A) is incorrect for the reasons just noted.

   Answer (B) is incorrect because the more foreseeable the act or omission, the more likely a court will be to rule that it was within the scope of risk. Here, the omissions appear to be reasonably foreseeable.

   Answer (C) is incorrect because the driver's conduct was not an intentional tort. The driver did not want a collision to occur, and did not know that a collision was substantially certain to happen. Finally, even if this was an intentional tort, that does not automatically mean the Bus Co. cannot be held liable; an employer may be liable for intentional torts if they are within the scope of employment.

201.   **Answer (D) is correct.** Even though Gilles' shot was in desperation, what he did was still something inherent in the game: fire a puck at high speed. And pucks fired at high speed often leave the ice and sometimes even fly into the stands. This is a risk inherent in attending a hockey game, and courts hold that spectators lose the right to sue for injuries caused by such a risk. Put differently, Gilles did not have a duty to refrain from hitting the puck into the stands during the game. This is considered by most courts to be a case of "primary" assumption of risk, and completely defeats recovery.

   Answer (A) is incorrect because nothing suggests that Gilles had substantial certainty that the puck would hit anyone if it did not go into the goal. This answer simply misreads the facts.

   Answer (B) is incorrect because "should have known with substantial certainty" is not sufficient to meet the intent requirement for battery.

Answer (C) is incorrect because the facts do not suggest that Gilles' shot was negligent. And even if it was, this is precisely the purpose of the primary assumption of risk doctrine. Gilles did not have a duty toward fans to refrain from negligently striking the puck.

202. **Answer (A) is correct.** The doctrine of primary assumption of risk operates regardless of the plaintiff's actual knowledge of the dangers she faces. Here, it is true that Vlad did not know that pucks could fly into the stands. But being hit by pucks flying into the stands is an inherent risk of attending a hockey game, and Vlad is held to "assume" that risk when he voluntarily attends the game. As a result, his claim is completely defeated. Had the barrier been shorter than those used by other teams, Vlad might have a reasonable argument that he did not assume the risk of being struck while in the seat he took, but the facts indicate that HockeyCo had constructed a barrier of the same height used in all other stadiums where professional hockey teams play.

Answer (B) is incorrect because the primary assumption of risk will completely defeat Vlad's claim, not provide a basis for reduction. HockeyCo did not owe Vlad a duty to prevent this accident from happening.

Answer (C) is incorrect because even if Vlad did not keep a lookout for flying pucks, there is no reason to address the comparative negligence issue. That is because there is no negligence of HockeyCo with which to compare Vlad's negligence.

Answer (D) is incorrect because, as explained above, the doctrine of primary assumption of risk applies to these facts.

203. **Answer (D) is correct.** An employee of a newspaper, through carelessness, caused an injurious false statement to be published.

Answer (A) is incorrect because the word "desiring" demonstrates the intent to do harm, and negligent defamation involves unintended harm.

Answer (B) is incorrect because the injury described is not actionable in defamation unless the statement was false, and answer (B) does not say that the statement was false.

Answer (C) is incorrect because Gabriel's defamation-by-omitting-praise contention is more far-fetched — one might say "paranoid" — than courts will accept. It is hard to see anything defamatory in this omission.

204. **Answer (C) is correct.** This was a game. The players impliedly consented to suffering apprehension of being touched. Thus, Steve was privileged to create the apprehension.

Answer (A) is incorrect because it fails to take account of Steve's privilege to create the apprehension in Rose.

Answer (B) is incorrect because "apprehension" exists even when the plaintiff knows she can avoid the contact. As the *Restatement* commentary states, apprehension is not the same as fear. Thus, if defendant aims a rock at the plaintiff, and plaintiff knows she can avoid being hit by ducking behind a door, plaintiff still has a valid assault claim because plaintiff knows she has to take this evasive action to avoid the contact. And it is wrong for defendant to place plaintiff in such a position. Here, plaintiff might have had a way to avoid contact, but she was still "apprehensive." (Of course, as noted above, Steve was privileged to create the apprehension, so there was no assault.)

Answer (D) is incorrect because we have enough facts to conclude that Steve is not liable for assault.

205.   **Answer (D) is correct.** Norm's conduct of driving 45 mph instead of 25 mph might have been unlawful, and he might be liable to Ronnie for negligence, but he did not intend to strike Ronnie. That is because he neither desired to strike her nor, *at a time when he could have done something to prevent striking her*, did he know to a substantial certainty that he would strike her. This is a negligence case, not a battery case.

Answer (A) is incorrect because intentionally driving the car is not the same as intentionally striking Ronnie, even if he knew at some point that he would in fact hit her.

Answer (B) is incorrect because "should have known the grave risk of striking a child" is not sufficient for battery. The intent required is either to desire contact or to know with substantial certainty that a contact will occur.

Answer (C) is incorrect because the "negligence per se" concept that is used to establish a duty in negligence law does not apply to the law of battery. It was unlawful to drive faster than 25 mph in that place, but Norm did not have the unlawful intent to strike Ronnie.

206.   **Answer (A) is correct.** Dan has claimed that Fortune's negligence consisted in the failure to build a stronger retaining wall. This is a question the jury must decide. Answer (A) informs the jury of its task.

Answer (B) is incorrect because it usurps the jury's function. Unless the facts are so clear that no reasonable jury could find that Fortune did not breach its duty, the court should leave the breach question to the jury.

Answer (C) is incorrect because reasonable care is not shown by proof that the defendant acted "in good faith and the best of its ability." The standard is objective; what would a reasonable person in the defendant's position have done.

Answer (D) is incorrect because it improperly cedes to the jury a question of law: whether a duty of care existed in this situation. The court should decide that question.

207. **Answer (C) is correct.** When a person undertakes to do something normally done by experts, reasonable care requires that she perform as well as a reasonable expert would have performed. (We don't want a layperson who tries to do a cosmetic nose job and botches it to argue that she did just as well as any normal layperson could have done.)

    Answer (A) is incorrect because the court must inform the jury of the proper standard, as well as certain types of information the jury may consider in determining whether the standard is met. Though the court should not try to sway the jury by communicating its view of the breach question, that is not what the court does when it tells the jury that defendant's conduct must be measured against the conduct of a reasonably skilled expert in these kinds of films.

    Answer (B) is incorrect because a party is not negligent simply because he tried something normally done by experts. Sometimes people get lucky and do as good a job as an expert. The issue is whether the conduct actually rose to that level.

    Answer (D) is incorrect because it misconstrues one important foundation of the "reasonable person" standard: that sometimes, it holds people to a level of care and skill that they are not able to meet. If a reasonable person would have avoided the harm, defendant breached her duty even if defendant was not capable of exercising that amount of care and skill.

208. **Answer (D) is correct.** Justice Blackburn set forth a standard that held a party strictly liable for keeping something on one's property that can do harm if it escapes. This is what happened here. The instruction states the essence of Blackburn's standard: if MotorCo's testing posed a substantial risk of harm to those outside its property as a result of the escape of one of its cars, MotorCo is strictly liable for the harm caused.

    Answer (A) is incorrect because this is not a case that fits into Blackburn's exception for "traffic on the highways." MotorCo was not engaging in normal highway traffic, and Potter did not voluntarily take to the road with MotorCo's experimental car.

    Answer (B) is incorrect because Justice Blackburn did not frame his standard in terms of the "non-natural" use of land. (It was Cairns in the House of Lords who stated that standard.)

    Answer (C) is incorrect because Justice Blackburn rejected this standard. As stated above, he viewed this as a case in which strict liability could be imposed.

209. **Answer (C) is correct.** Recovery on an "abnormally dangerous activity" theory requires proof that the type of harm suffered was caused by a feature of the activity that made it abnormally dangerous. Here, that feature was the explosiveness of the fuel (greater than the explosiveness of regular automobile fuels). Because the harm was caused by a collision with Potter's car, and not by an explosion, MotorCo is not strictly liable.

Answer (A) is incorrect because it fails to account for the requirement that the harm be caused by the "abnormally dangerous" feature of the activity.

Answer (B) is incorrect because it assumes that if the balance of social benefit against risk favors the benefit, MotorCo may not be held liable. This is not correct. The six-part standard set forth in *Restatements (Second) of Torts* § 520 is not a categorical test; an activity need not meet each element. The court is to view the activity as a whole in light of all the elements, and decide whether it qualifies. Thus, even an activity the benefit of which outweighs the risk it creates can qualify as abnormally dangerous.

Answer (D) is incorrect because it has the element backward. Under the *Restatement* test, if the harm can be prevented by the exercise of reasonable care, it is *less* likely that it will qualify as abnormally dangerous.

210. Most courts hold that violation of a licensing statute is not negligence per se. This is because such a statute does not set forth a specific standard of conduct against which a person's behavior is to be measured. Rather, it merely provides that one must possess a license to do particular things. This does not mean that Snape will not be held liable; on the contrary, his duty will be to drive as well as a reasonable licensed driver. But the statute is not the source of his duty. Some courts, following the view of the *Restatement (Second) of Torts*, hold that violation of a licensing statute is some evidence of negligence.

211. **Answer (D) is correct.** Even if Sharon was mentally ill, she could still be found comparatively negligent for walking onto the highway. The facts will have to be investigated, of course, but this claim seems viable.

Answer (A) is incorrect because defendants did have a duty to inform Serene Chateau of Sharon's tendencies. The state was in a special relationship with Sharon. This imposed a duty of reasonable care for her safety. A reasonable social worker would have realized that Sharon presented certain risks to herself that might not be apparent to the new facility, at least for a while. Reasonable care toward Sharon therefore would require informing Serene Chateau of her tendency to walk away and become disoriented.

Answer (B) is incorrect because a jury is very likely to find that defendants breached their duty. There is nothing in the facts to suggest a cognizable excuse for their failure to inform Serene Chateau of Sharon's tendencies.

Answer (C) is incorrect because the failure to notify Serene Chateau of Sharon's tendencies was almost certainly a "but-for" cause of Sharon's harm. That is, it is very likely that had the state notified Serene Chateau of the relevant facts, the facility would have taken steps to monitor Sharon more carefully, and perhaps limit her freedom to leave the facility.

212. **Answer (B) is correct.** The "directness" approach to proximate cause basically asks whether any harm was reasonably foreseeable from defendant's conduct, and if so, whether the

chain of events from the negligent act to the harm was unbroken (direct). Answer (B) states that test.

Answer (A) is incorrect because the "directness" approach does not require that the harm that occurred be what one might expect. In fact, an important feature of the approach as articulated by Andrews and the decisions of the courts of which Andrews approved is that the type of harm that actually occurs is of minor, if any, importance.

Answer (C) is incorrect because even under a "directness" approach, the plaintiff's own negligence does not cut off the liability of the originally negligent actor, especially if it was reasonably foreseeable (as was the case here).

Answer (D) is incorrect because it states a risk-type of approach, not a directness approach.

213. **Answer (A) is correct.** Scope of risk approaches tend to look at whether the victim was within a class of persons to whom harm was reasonably foreseeable, and at whether the type of harm that occurred was of the kind one might reasonably expect. Answer (A) embodies these principles.

Answer (B) is incorrect because courts do not require that the precise chain of events have been reasonably foreseeable. Even rather convoluted chains of events can be considered within the scope of risk created by the defendant's carelessness if the victim and type of harm the victim suffered were reasonably foreseeable. (Note that the same is true in courts using a directness approach; the precise manner in which the harm comes about need not be reasonably foreseeable.)

Answer (C) is incorrect because it states a directness type of test rather than a scope of risk test.

Answer (D) is incorrect because courts do not require the *extent* of injury to be reasonably foreseeable. (Note that the same is true under a directness approach.)

214. **Answer (B) is correct.** According to *Restatement (Second) of Torts*, in order to be liable the land possessor must know or have reason to know that a trespasser is actually present.

Answer (A) is incorrect because there is no reason to suppose that Tommy assumed any risk.

Answer (C) is incorrect because Muskrat owed Tommy no duty.

Answer (D) is incorrect because foreseeability of a trespasser's presence is insufficient to support liability.

215. **Answer (C) is correct.** Most likely, Lois's entry onto Peter's property was justified by the doctrine of private necessity. A person has a privilege to commit what would otherwise be

a trespass if the action appears necessary to prevent imminent harm to person or property. That was Lois's reason for entering Peter's land. She had reason to believe that the child was injured and needed help. Thus, she was not a trespasser.

Answer (A) is incorrect because Lois's entry was voluntary. She was not coerced into going onto the property.

Answer (B) is incorrect because, as explained above, Lois was not a trespasser. (Note also that if she was a trespasser but did not physical harm to the property, Lois would be liable for nominal damages; physical harm is not an element of the tort of trespass.)

Answer (D) is incorrect because, as explained above, Lois was not a trespasser.

216. False light. The false light claim is similar to defamation, except that under false light doctrine the statement can be actionable even if it is true, whereas for defamation it cannot be actionable unless it is false. Other elements are held in common: the false light must be offensive (similar to defamation's criterion of "harmful to the plaintiff's reputation") and the defendant must have publicized (cf. "published") the communication. Because the standard for false light is more inclusive, many defamation claims can be actionable as false light claims as well.

217. **Answer (C) is correct.** Filbert bought a ticket to a particular destination, as did the other passengers. Though one can understand Filbert's anxiety after the engine blowout and desire to land at a closer airport, there was in fact no need to divert the plane. Thus, the airline's refusal, which kept Filbert confined for longer than he wanted to be, was not unlawful.

Answer (A) is incorrect because there *was* confinement. As explained above, it was not unlawful, but Filbert was certainly confined.

Answer (B) is incorrect because it makes no sense. The other passengers would not be falsely imprisoned by landing at a closer airport. In fact, their confinement on the plane would end sooner than if they proceeded to the original destination.

Answer (D) is incorrect because physical harm is not an element of false imprisonment, as long as the victim knows of the confinement (and Filbert is well aware of it in this situation).

218. **Answer (C) is correct.** Most American courts hold that physicians are only required to reveal information that a reasonable person in the patient's position would have considered material in deciding whether to have the surgery. This does not give each patient the greatest right of self-determination, but it is a realistic standard that avoids requiring the physician to reveal a huge amount of information that most people simply would not consider important.

Answer (A) is incorrect because one of the physician's obligations is to reveal possible side effects of the surgery. Patients consider this information to be important as they consider their options.

Answer (B) is incorrect because the success of Kevin's case does not depend on a weighing of the benefits of the surgery against the harm it did to Kevin. True, Kevin must have suffered harm as a result of the doctor's failure to disclose material information, but the mere fact that the surgery was otherwise successful does not exonerate McAllister from the possibility he might be liable for the pain and suffering Kevin endured as a result of the side-effects.

Answer (D) is incorrect because most American courts do not allow medical custom to set the standard for proper disclosure in informed consent cases.

219.   **Answer (D) is correct.** Most courts allow a narrow exception to the informed consent standard. If the physician reasonably believes that this particular patient is so sensitive that providing certain information will cause such anxiety that it actually will harm the patient, then the physician need not provide that information.

Answer (A) is incorrect because, as explained above, a narrow exception allows the physician to withhold information if she reasonably believes the patient will be harmed by the anxiety caused by that information.

Answer (B) is incorrect because it fails to take account of the exception.

Answer (C) is incorrect because it grossly overstates the applicability of the exception. A doctor may not withhold information merely because she thinks the patient will make the "wrong" decision if the information is provided. Such an exception would overwhelm the patient-centered informed consent standard.

220.   **Answer (B) is correct.** Courts tend to hedge on the causation issue. If courts wished to give the greatest effect to a patient's right of self-determination, they would establish a causation standard that would be met by proof that this particular patient would not have agreed to the surgery if he had been told about the possible side-effects that occurred. Thus, even if a reasonable patient would have agreed to the procedure, the plaintiff could prevail. But courts have chosen instead to establish an objective test of causation: plaintiff must prove that a reasonable person would not have undergone the procedure if she had known of these possible side effects.

One reason courts adopt the objective standard is that the subjective standard would be too easy to meet. A patient who has suffered horribly would almost always believe, in hindsight, that she would not have agreed to the procedure had she known this might happen. But that might not always be true as a matter of foresight; a patient told that she will benefit from a particular procedure might choose to undergo the procedure even if she knows that certain side effects might occur. Answer (B) is correct because it states the objective standard.

Answer (A) is incorrect for the reasons just given.

Answer (C) is incorrect because it deals with the problem of proximate cause or scope of liability, not cause in fact.

Answer (D) is incorrect because proof of duty and breach does not establish causation. In a negligence case, the plaintiff must also prove that the breach caused harm.

221. **Answer (D) is correct.** Most courts hold that when two negligent agencies combine to cause damage, and either force standing alone would have been sufficient to cause all of the harm, the parties responsible for both agencies are treated as causes of the harm, and are jointly and severally liable for it. If one of the agencies of harm is not attributable to negligence, the party responsible for the other force is liable for the full extent of the harm. Here, the facts indicate that Wingnut City negligently maintained the dam, and that the water from the dam would have been sufficient by itself to cause all of Abel's harm. Thus, Wingnut City is liable for all of the harm.

Answer (A) is incorrect for the reasons just stated.

Answer (B) is incorrect because, as long as either force would have been sufficient to cause all of the damage, it does not matter if more water from the river flood reached Abel's gallery than from the dam.

Answer (C) is incorrect because, as stated above, Wingnut City is liable for all of the harm.

222. Wingnut City has a reasonable argument that it should only be liable for the value of any goods Abel could have saved if he had had an extra hour to remove some of his goods from the building. The analogy is to the wrongful death of a person who, due to other factors, had only a short time to live. Here, some of Abel's goods were about to be destroyed by the river water. Thus, Wingnut City may argue that it is only liable for the value of any goods Abel would not have had time to save. Note that the court might not accept this idea. After all, Wingnut City *did* destroy all of the art. In addition, such an argument is not availing in the previous case, where an argument by Wingnut City that it should not be responsible because Abel's goods would have been destroyed anyway was not considered valid. The outcome is not clear.

223. In this toxic tort case, Platt must prove two things to prove cause in fact: *First*, Platt must prove that it is more likely than not that the chemical that leaked from the tank *was capable of causing* this type of cancer. *Second*, Platt must prove that it is more likely than not that the chemical *actually did cause* Platt's case of cancer. This, in turn, will require Platt to show that the chemical reached his property (perhaps through ground water), and that it

reached his body and caused the disease. Much of Platt's proof might have to be in statistical form, and, of course, he will need expert testimony to establish both basic points.

224. **Answer (C) is correct.** By participating in the game of tag, Rose impliedly consented to what might otherwise be assaults. She also impliedly consented to certain contacts that might otherwise constitute batteries. She did not consent to a harmful fall onto the street. If Steve intended to make Rose fall into the street, therefore, he can be liable for battery. Here, Steve might not have *desired* Rose to fall into the street, but if he *knew* to a substantial certainty that she would fall, he can be liable for battery because she did fall. The contact, of course, did not have to be direct. It is sufficient if Steve caused Rose to fall into the street with the stated intention.

    Answer (A) is incorrect because, as explained above, Steve did possess the requisite intent if he knew to a substantial certainty that Rose would fall.

    Answer (B) is incorrect because the privilege to touch Rose did not give Steve a privilege to cause the kind of contact Rose suffered.

    Answer (D) is incorrect because "should have known to a substantial certainty" is not sufficient to establish intent for battery. What is required is desire to contact or *actual knowledge* that the contact is substantially certain to occur.

225. **Answer (A) is correct.** Ludwig possessed the intent required for assault. He drove toward Viola, while able to avoid her, with knowledge that she saw him coming and that he would hit her if she did not get out of the way (the "substantial certainty" arm of intent). Thus, he "intended" to cause apprehension of imminent harmful or offensive contact. According to the doctrine of transferred intent, his intent to commit assault would "transfer" to a battery claim if he struck Viola, which he did.

    Answer (B) is incorrect because "should have known the grave risk of striking a child" is not sufficient for battery. The intent required is either to desire contact or to know with substantial certainty that a contact will occur.

    Answer (C) is incorrect because the "negligence per se" concept that is used to establish a duty in negligence law does not apply to the law of battery. It was unlawful to drive faster than 25 mph in that place, but Ludwig did not have the unlawful intent to strike Viola.

    Answer (D) is incorrect because, as discussed above, Ludwig did possess the intent for assault, which transfers to battery.

226. The two torts overlap most frequently where the defendant's behavior combines "outrage" and "intrusion." Stalking might give rise to both claims. When the defendant has power over the plaintiff and can control her mobility to some extent — for instance, the defendant might be a high school principal and the plaintiff a high school student; the defendant might be an

employer and the plaintiff an employee — both claims could arise when the defendant repeatedly hounds the plaintiff with intimate, personal questions.

227.   **Answer (D) is correct**. Many courts hold that one who has a special relationship with a dangerous person has an obligation to warn potential victims of the dangerous person of that person's intention to cause them harm. Some courts require that the threat of harm be specific as to the victim, but the facts of this problem indicate that the threat was to a specific victim. Ambrosia may be held liable for failing to warn the victim, call the police, or take other reasonable steps.

Answer (A) is incorrect because a jury would be justified in finding that Ambrosia's failure to act was a cause in fact of the murder. Unless the facts show otherwise, it is reasonable to conclude that had she provided a reasonable warning, the killing could have been prevented.

Answer (B) is incorrect because, even if Ambrosia has no duty to "control" her son's acts, she does have a duty to warn, as explained above.

Answer (C) is incorrect because intervening criminal conduct does not necessarily cut off the liability of the negligent actor. Especially where the criminal conduct is reasonably foreseeable (as it appears to be here), the negligent actor may be held responsible.

228.   *Criticism*: Many people do not read warnings. Some people read warnings but misinterpret the information conveyed. If warnings proliferate, perhaps consumers would suffer from "information overload" and become unable to absorb everything warned about. Some warnings state the obvious. *Critique of the criticism*: If consumers process warnings ineffectively, that might mean that sellers should figure out how to warn more effectively, rather than just escape liability. Warnings can convey not only news of a risk but ways to reduce the risk — helpful information that the user might not know. The effort to compose a warning makes a product seller keep dangers in mind, and might foster safety-related innovation.

INDEX